T.J. JUMPER

Jump and Shout

Lessons Learned on the Path to a High School State Championship

First published by Thomas Jae Publishing 2022

Copyright © 2022 by T.J. Jumper

All rights reserved. No part of this publication may be reproduced, stored or transmitted in any form or by any means, electronic, mechanical, photocopying, recording, scanning, or otherwise without written permission from the publisher. It is illegal to copy this book, post it to a website, or distribute it by any other means without permission.

T.J. Jumper asserts the moral right to be identified as the author of this work.

T.J. Jumper has no responsibility for the persistence or accuracy of URLs for external or third-party Internet Websites referred to in this publication and does not guarantee that any content on such Websites is, or will remain, accurate or appropriate.

First edition

ISBN: 978-0-578-36968-6

Editing by Taylor Pensoneau
Cover art by Walter Cueva

This book was professionally typeset on Reedsy.
Find out more at reedsy.com

This book is dedicated:

To my parents and my sister for all of their continuous support, time and energy to help me achieve my dreams and become the person I am today.

To my lovely wife, thank you for all you do for our family.

To my children, you can do anything you put your mind too.

To Coach Garcia for all you did for me. You are not only a great coach, but also a great person. Your positive impact on your athletes and students is simply amazing

Contents

Foreword   iii
Preface   vii
Acknowledgement   x

I   Part One

Chapter 1	3
Early Elementary	3
Chapter 2	7
Late Elementary	7
Chapter 3	13
Middle School Years	13
Chapter 4	24
Ninth Grade	24
Chapter 5	34
Tenth Grade	34
Chapter 6	47
Eleventh Grade	47
Chapter 7	60
Senior Year	60

II Part Two

Chapter 8	77
Balance of the Four "Musts"	77
Chapter 9	83
Characteristic One: Drive	83
Chapter 10	89
Characteristic Two: Commitment	89
Chapter 11	92
Characteristic Three: Determination	92
Chapter 12	95
Characteristic Four: Mindset X2	95
Conclusion	100
Notes	102
Also by T.J. Jumper	103

Foreword

When T.J. first shared with me that he was putting together a book for young athletes, I was finishing my first semester of medical school, buried deep in the stress of classes. I did not realize it at the time, but I was longing for something to pull me back into the world of athletics. Hanging up my softball cleats was, and still is, one of the most difficult things I have done in my life. So, needless to say I was more than excited to read his story, take in his message, and be a part of his writing journey.

Many years ago, my family lived in the same neighborhood as the Jumper family, and T.J. was simply the dad of three adorable girls that my friend and I absolutely loved playing with. One day, we played a wiffleball game in their backyard where I got my first glance at T.J.'s athleticism, which led to me learning all about his athletic background. My relationship with their family grew, and I ended up babysitting their daughters every so often. When I entered high school, I thought everything would change as T.J. was now Dr. Jumper, my principal. I did not think I would see anymore of the fun, energetic T.J. I knew playing wiffle ball in the backyard. If you know T.J. in any way, you would laugh at that misconception. In fact, I can say I never saw him walking the halls without a smile on his face.

High school went on, and I managed to stay out of his office. However, I knew it could not have gone that smoothly. On one of my last days of school, I walked into a small classroom to give my Capstone speech, a speech I spent a large part of the year preparing. Presenting this speech was the last box to check off before graduation, and when I walked into the room, I was surprised to see T.J. sitting there ready to hear what I had to say. Instantly, my level of nervousness rose, as I thought very highly of him. Plus, my speech was largely influenced by my own athletic career, specifically with track and field, an area he is well-versed in. However, I should have known better. After I finished speaking, we had an authentic conversation about the next phase in my life. I left feeling empowered, which speaks to how much he cares about his students and their journeys.

Reflecting on T.J.'s story, I realized he is just like you and me, like most people who will read this book. A genuine, hardworking, Midwesterner with natural athletic ability who found joy in sports. However, he found a way to set himself apart from his fellow competitors and that is what he brings to you through "Jump and Shout." He gives an honest and accurate portrayal of what it is like participating in multiple sports, club sports, high school athletics, etc., and all the logistics and decisions that come into play. Most importantly though, he shares with his readers how to maximize one's potential and their experiences to achieve their goals, whatever they may be. He provides great insight into the decisions and factors that come into play, such as the role of academics and school choice, injuries and mental well-being, playing multiple sports versus committing to one or two, and individual responsibility and autonomy.

As you read his story and his message, my biggest hope is that you can develop an appreciation for how much of the athletic journey is shaped by the individual and their ability to develop their autonomy. Pursuing excellence in athletics is simply a different way of life. There will be plenty of sacrifices made. I remember many times when I had to say no to my friends, miss out on spring break trips, and be mindful of what I was putting into my body and how I was sleeping. I am not saying it was an all the time thing, nor did I have to give up my social life. There were just times when I had to take it upon myself to choose me, my teammates, and my sport over other things. Competing at a high level in athletics requires a level of commitment where it becomes a part of your daily routine. In college, I would often schedule my study sessions into my day, and guess what? I also scheduled in my hitting sessions that I would do outside of practice. I never missed a session that I scheduled into my planner. It became a part of my day-to-day life just like my classes.

As I sit here, thinking about what T.J. wrote and what he has accomplished in life, I realized I missed out on a great resource during my college years. In high school, he was always open about his athletic career and shared many stories, which I enjoyed, but it is difficult as a teenager to really appreciate how much others can help you along your journey. By picking up this book, regardless of where you are in your athletic career, you will be gaining knowledge, wisdom, and insight that I wish I had during my athletic career, especially my collegiate career. T.J brings with him the experience of being a consistently excellent high jumper, of battling through the emotional, mental, and physical toll that injuries bring and returning to an even higher level of competition, and of performing against the stiffest competition as a Division I track and field athlete. Once his own athletic career was over, he continued as a coach while building up his expertise even more. And now, 25 years since he won his state high jump title, he is still finding ways to help young athletes reach their potential as he launched Jumper Athletics with his wife, Laura Jumper, and his father, Jim Jumper.

And let us not lose sight of the end goal. T.J. shares his "Jump and Shout" moment not for himself, but rather to help empower and inspire his readers and the athletes that he works with to achieve their own "Jump and Shout" moment. I know from my own "Jump and Shout" moment, winning the 2019 Division II Softball National Championship, that there is no better feeling. It is hard to put it into words, but it is worth the effort as T.J. will illustrate for you.

~ Kendall Cornick
2021 NCAA Woman of the Year
2022 NCAA Today's Top Ten Honoree
Division II Softball All-American

Preface

Growing up many kids develop childhood dreams and have visions of a successful life. Unfortunately, sometimes these dreams fail to be achieved. Fortunately, through many trials, tribulations and lessons I was able to achieve my childhood dream of winning an Illinois High School Association (IHSA) State Championship. Very few high school athletes become a state champion. Most people in the town I grew up in, including myself, thought that if there was a chance to win a state title that it would be through basketball, but that was not the case. The childhood dream of winning a state high school title occurred while I was a senior at Springfield Lanphier High School when I won the 1996 high school class AA (large school) state championship in the high jump at the IHSA Illinois State Track and Field Championships at Eastern Illinois University.

The title *Jump and Shout* comes from the headline used by the *State Journal Register* newspaper's sports page that brought the story "Jump and Shout: T.J. Wins" to the readers of Springfield and the surrounding area of my winning the high jump state championship. The headline *"Jump and Shout"* described my actions after clearing the high jump bar late in the competition at each of the heights of 6'8", 6'9", 6'10", and 6'11". These actions of clearing the bar, landing on the mat, getting to my feet, and screaming with my arms flexed and fists clenched in front of me resulted from my emotions and excitement. The emotions were the product of failures in previous years, none bigger than the situation that developed at the state track meet in 1995, my junior year.

Jump and Shout describes the excitement and emotions one feels when he/she achieves his/her dreams and/or achieves a high level of success. These emotions come from overcoming trials, tribulations and failures on the road to achieving success. Each individual has his/her own dream and idea of ultimate success, the emotional high after achieving the "*Jump and Shout*" moment. Although this book focuses on one "Jump and Shout" moment, I have had several throughout my life so far. The book is in chronological order from my early life to the one big moment as there were multiple life experiences and lessons learned throughout the years that led up to my senior year of high school. The hope for this book is to share my path and the lessons I learned on my journey so that others can achieve their own "*Jump and Shout*" moment and also achieve high amounts of success in athletics and/or life. Although the book is written based on my high jump success, the lessons learned apply to any athlete in any sport.

The book is structured with the idea that in order for one to understand the lessons learned and be able to put them into action, an understanding of the background and the build up to my "Jump and Shout" moment is needed. This is Part I of the book. The lessons learned resulted in being prepared to be at the highest levels of mental/emotional, physical, tactical, and technical abilities to achieve a great outcome. I titled these the four "Musts." In order to be consistent at the four "Musts", an athlete needs to possess the four characteristics to achieve high success. I also added the idea that this preparation of the four "Musts" and the four characteristics for high success allows an athlete to be consistently excellent. This information is shared in Part II of the book. Some say to achieve high success or a state title that you have to have a little luck. Unfortunately, through forty years of competing in multiple sports and watching others compete, my feeling is that most people are not prepared to achieve such luck because they are missing some portion of the characteristics to achieve high success or have not optimized the four "Musts". The purpose of this book is for more athletes to be prepared to utilize that luck through possessing and implementing the characteristics to achieve and high success and utilizing the four "Musts to achieve their "*Jump and Shout*" moment.

The Roman philosopher Seneca once said "Luck is what happens when preparation meets opportunity."

*There is a free worksheet that goes along with the "*Jump and Shout*" book. The worksheet follows the reader's self-reflections at the end of each chapter and will help you make an action plan to achieve your goals. To receive your free worksheet, go to the Jumper Athletics website at https://tjjumper.com/ and click on the "book" tab. Below the "*Jump and Shout*" click on the link that says "worksheet", input your email and the free worksheet will be emailed to you.

Acknowledgement

A huge special thank you to Kendall Cornick for all of your extra time assisting me with the book and for agreeing to write such an amazing forward to the book. I am so proud of you for all of your accomplishments, what you will achieve in the future, and for who you are as a person.

I

Part One

The story of T.J. Jumper's path from an early age to his "Jump and Shout" moment of winning a high school state championship.

Part One

Chapter 1

Early Elementary

I, T.J. Jumper, was the second child born after older sister Michelle to Marilyn and Jim Jumper in a small western Illinois town. A couple years after being born we moved to Lincoln, Illinois and then to Springfield, Illinois, all before I was seven years old. My mom would become a school secretary and my father would be a junior high school teacher and basketball coach in the small town of Elkhart, just north of Springfield. My dad also would end up coaching multiple sports, the main sport being basketball, and teach at the high school in the same district, Mt. Pulaski.

I attended two years of preschool because I had a late fall birthday and one year of kindergarten. As a young child, my teachers would describe me as having a lot of energy. The preschool and kindergarten teacher who saw me later at a basketball game as a high school senior stated, "My memory of you is looking out the window at school during parent-teacher conferences and seeing you jump up and down on the roof of your parents car." During parent-teacher conferences, my parents would typically hear about my struggles with beginning to read and fidgetiness in class.

T.J. as a young child playing basketball on the driveway with the family dog.

Early elementary school would see more of the same when we moved to Springfield. My sister and I attended a small private school. I would be an average to just below average student through fourth grade. I was routinely in trouble at school because of my boundless energy and unwillingness to sit still in class. Many times I would find myself in lunch detention from being warned too many times to sit down and stop talking.

The positive during this time was that my parents introduced me to sports. I was introduced to soccer, participated in baseball, and played biddy-ball basketball. My parents even put me into one winter of gymnastics tumbling. Practicing and playing sports was where I was the happiest. I did not care what sport it was. As long as there was competition, I was content. On one report card a teacher commented, "If T.J. would spend as much energy with his academics, especially his reading, as he does at recess he would be a great student." The games of choice at recess were kickball and soccer. Many times the teachers would ask me to not play so hard at recess. I would get put into recess time out because I was playing so hard or because I had grass stains on my school uniform.

If I was not at a team practice or playing games at night or on the weekends, I was outside playing sports with the other older neighborhood boys (Mike, JP, and Tim) or attending the games my dad was coaching. One year, one of my dad's teams went to the Illinois Elementary School Association state basketball tournament and I was the ball boy. This is where my dream of playing in the state high school basketball tournament began. Over the years, my dad would take me to high school games and to the state basketball and baseball tournaments, which only enhanced my dream of playing at the state tournament.

The darkest days came in third and fourth grade because I felt I was always in trouble and that I was different from my classmates. This is also when the teachers provided a reading assessment to my entire class and I knew I did not do well. Afterwards, the teachers informed my parents that they believed that I had a reading disability. I was sent every other day from the small private school to a public school for part of the day to receive extra reading support while the rest of my class stayed at school and learned other things.

After not seeing much improvement, my parents enrolled me at Sylvan Learning ©. The first few sessions were assessment driven. The results showed that as a reader I read for comprehension, but was slow at fluency (speed at which I read). After about a year of tutoring on fluency and extra work at home with my parents, my reading scores increased and were above grade-level for comprehension and fluency. Reading was no longer an issue or a weakness.

What I learned

1. At an early age I learned what I was passionate about. Although this would change and be added to over time.
2. What my strengths and weaknesses were, which ebbed and flowed over time.
3. How to overcome a weakness through hard work and focus.

Reader self-reflection

1. What are you passionate about? What do you love to do?
2. What do you do to ensure you have time to follow your passions?
3. What are your strengths and weaknesses?
4. How will you go about addressing those weaknesses?
5. How will you go about keeping your strengths?

Chapter 2

Late Elementary

After the struggle of third and fourth grade, along with the extra tutoring, my parents decided to have me attend fifth and sixth grade in the Springfield Public Schools. I attended Feitshans fifth and sixth grade center, and it ended up being one of the best decisions my parents made in my childhood. In fifth grade, I started to become an average to just above average student. Then in sixth grade I earned straight A's on my report card for the first time ever. The teachers I had at Feitshans worked to meet my learning needs and the focus was on progress. The teachers discovered my passion and connected sports to my learning while at the same time building a relationship with me. Each of the teachers came to at least one sporting event I competed in during those two years.

I was fortunate to have an amazing teacher to teach me math for two years in a row. Miss Halford took a great deal of interest in me as a person and in my learning. She made learning fun and was invested in her students. One day she called me up to her desk to show me my test score after she had recently watched me play in a basketball game. The words that came from her have stuck with me to this day, "T.J., you can do anything you put your mind to, you will be as successful in whatever you decide to do." I used to hate school, but during this two-year time period I started to enjoy attending school and my self-confidence quickly rose.

During this same two-year period, my father had two major conversations with me. Both conversations motivated me to want to play college basketball and earn a scholarship. In fifth grade, my dad mentioned that it would be great if I could find a way to earn a scholarship for college. In sixth grade, the second major conversation occurred and was related to how I was being fairly successful in athletics at an early age. He said that "to be a champion you have to be a champion in all phases of your life." This was a turning point for me to improve academically and as a person. There were also a few conversations about how college coaches looked at academic grades and the characteristics of a person they were thinking of recruiting. More was required to getting a college scholarship than simply being a successful athlete. These conversations were highly motivating for me and was the time that the idea of working hard in school and on the athletic court clicked.

At the same time, I met several of my closest friends during this two-year time period at school and through sports. School basketball started in fifth grade and the school was big enough that we had two teams. We practiced at school and then played games on Saturdays during the winter months at the Springfield Boys and Girls Club. Having a coach who was not my father allowed me to learn to be coachable and how to handle tough feedback. Basketball was my biggest love as I would spend Sundays doing school work with my dad at his school's open gyms and attending his team's games.

CHAPTER 2

T.J. in his Feitshan's basketball uniform

Although basketball was my love during the late elementary years, another sport, soccer, occupied most of my time. I played competitive soccer with teammates from all over the Springfield and surrounding area. We practiced approximately three times a week and played in tournaments during the fall, spring, and summer. The team also did some indoor soccer training during the winter. The enjoyment of the game was taken away from me during sixth grade when the soccer team added a former college player to be the coach. His style of coaching was to yell, be sarcastic, and to play mean. He yelled at me in one game to stop smiling. The smiling was not from goofing around, but for the love of competing. During the spring season, I was pulled from being a starter as a striker and was never given a reason why. During this time as a substitute, I was subbed into the game the last portion of a half, after we were losing, or when we needed a goal.

During this time, I was going through some social-emotional growth. There were many trials and tribulations related to soccer as I felt the coach did not like me. I was running a busy schedule of sports that were going well (basketball and baseball), but the interactions with the soccer coach were causing me to have negative emotions. There were many nights of tears as I felt lost and that I could not do anything right. Multiple conversations occurred in the car ride home from tournaments with me being frustrated and crying and my mother and father having stern talks with me. The focus of the talks were related to if I was doing everything I could to improve and win the starting spot back.

I can recall a specific conversation, a tough one for me, related to how I mentally prepared to play my best. The reason for this came about because two of my friends on the team and I between games decided to play sand soccer in the sun and heat in between games. Another time, the three of us boys were running around our room jumping between beds and then playing a game with a ball where we tried to block each other from scoring. We were drenched in sweat and winded by the time my dad came into the room and made us stop. We were clearly not at our physical best for the game a little later in the day.

During this turbulent time, I was challenged to learn how to mentally, emotionally, and physically prepare to compete in a very basic manner. The uneasiness, heartbreak, and negative feelings brought about by the situation I was in with competitive soccer along with the tough conversations from my parents taught me to think about how I could get a competitive advantage and be more prepared to consistently put my best foot forward. The hardest conversation came when my parents asked me if I thought I was good enough to be starting. I did believe I was the better player and that I was getting robbed by not being in the starting line-up.

My parents challenged me to be better technically. I had to be so good that the coach had no other choice, but to play me more. I was asked what I was willing to do for this to happen. After my parents facilitated me thinking through my schedule, I started waking up early before school two to three days a week to work on my dribbling and trapping skills. My sister and I also developed a "nut meg" game where if you dribbled around someone you received one point, and if you "nut megged" the person you got two points. A "nut meg" is when you put the ball between the defenders legs and go around them and get the ball. I followed this plan for about a month until the end of soccer season. I did become technically better, but it did not lead me to a starting position by the end of the season.

Lessons learned

1. What I put in my mind, I can do.
2. Developed confidence in myself.
3. Learned being a champion was not a sometimes thing, but an all the time thing and that mentality should be in everything that you do. Commit to the process.
4. How to prepare to compete at a higher level consistently.
5. If you don't like your circumstances, work to overcome them.

Reader self-reflection

1. Are you meeting your potential academically, physically, mentally, socially, technically (skill), and tactically (in game knowledge and philosophy)?
2. What do you do on a daily basis to set yourself up for success?
3. How can you evaluate your circumstances and figure out what you need to improve?
4. Who can you turn to for help? Who can you have honest conversations with?

Chapter 3

Middle School Years

Going into seventh grade, I was as confident as ever with life, school and sports. Some tough decisions of what I was going to focus on had to be made in the fall. What I was not aware of was how a new sport would enter in and change my path forever. Over the summer before seventh grade, I played baseball and played in open gyms at Lanphier High School for basketball, attended basketball camps, and played picked-up basketball games.

At the start of August, I had to make a decision of where I was going to spend my time because school sports were going to be starting and more intense than what was experienced in fifth and sixth grade. Therefore, I decided to give up competitive soccer and just play recreational soccer in the fall so I had more time to work on basketball and baseball. I enjoyed soccer, but basketball was my true love and I was starting to see some real improvement as a baseball pitcher. I felt so confident with basketball, that at "Almost 7th grade Night" at Washington Middle School, I met Mr. Howard. He was the basketball coach and introduced me as his starting point guard. As coach and I were talking I caught a glimpse of the trophy case in the foyer, and told him I thought we could have a pretty good team. That night I imagined the day of opening that trophy case and placing a trophy in it for state basketball.

Washington Middle School was considered an inner city school that was located on the southeast side of town. Many would describe the area as diverse with middle-to-low socio-economic families . It was known to be a tough school with discipline issues involving lots of fights. The Springfield School District lists the current day makeup of the school to be just over 70 percent free-reduced lunch with a school break down approximately 44 percent white, 44 percent black, and just over 8 percent as other. As I reflect back, I was so fortunate to go to Washington as I went to school with some of my best friends, and had an amazing two years of school. I was academically challenged, had great teachers and school administrators, and was able to get all A's and B's for grades. Many life lessons were also learned.

The fall soccer season went well. I was on a winning soccer recreational soccer team and continued working on my skills. I worked one to two days a week on my soccer trapping, dribbling and shooting. I was fortunate to score many goals that fall and get into great shape while also working on my basketball skills with my dad. My dad firmly believed that it was good to be a multi-sport athlete as it physically prepared you for the next sport and also gave your mind a break.

As early November came around, basketball tryouts for the school basketball team occurred. The team was amazing. We had some of my best friends along with two future NCAA Division 1 players in Victor Chuckwudebe and Jeff Walker. We were an extremely close team and had a lot of talent. We had speed and height. Most games were blowout victories where the starters played the first half and the substitutes played the second half. The city started to take notice and the crowd sizes were getting bigger and bigger. All of the city high school varsity coaches watched at least one if not more games. In Illinois, there is a sports association for middle schools called Illinois Elementary School Association (IESA). The IESA holds a state series just like the high school sport's associations. Our seventh grade team went undefeated on the season and also won the Illinois IESA state tournament for large schools. Our vision had been achieved, and we put a state championship trophy in the school's trophy case.

The Washington 7th grade IESA State Basketball Championship picture. T.J. Jumper is #31.

My confidence was at an all time high. The only negative during the winter that I was dealing with was a rumor going around school about my sexuality because I had told a couple girls I was not going to date them. I was too focused on sports and felt I did not have enough time for a girlfriend. No one was above the rumor mill, and I like many were victims of it. I was routinely asked about my sexuality from classmates at school and on the bus. The rumors bothered me some. I hoped that they would eventually go away if I just denied them and pretended it did not bother me. I refused to allow the rumors to distract me from what I wanted. Later in the school year, I would have my first girlfriend who was an eighth grader. I had met her after basketball practices on the activity bus home and later heard she liked me. She played basketball on the eighth grade team so we had a similar interest. We sat together on the activity bus on the way home and then started dating. I quickly learned how to balance talking on the phone with my girlfriend, getting my school work completed, and participating in basketball.

As the spring came around, my friends talked about going out for the school's track and field team. I originally had no plans to run track because I was starting to become more focused on baseball. My dad was concerned about the time commitment and the upcoming baseball season. We had some tough conversations, but I begged my parents to go out for track to be with my friends and just have a sport that I played for fun. There were no expectations of me being good at track.

Mr. Howard, who was the seventh grade basketball coach, was also the school's boys' track coach. There were no tryouts as everyone who wanted to participate could. Coach introduced all the field events and let anyone try any event in practice if they wished after he introduced them. One day, he introduced the high jump in the gym and then we went outside and tried the long jump. During that first week, we also ran a 100-meter sprint time trial and then a one-mile time trial. The coach would then ask us to list two or three events we would like to do.

For most of the meets, I ran the 100-meter hurdles and long jumped. Occasionally I would run on some sprint relays. In these events I typically placed in the top eight at the bigger invites and would be second through fourth at the smaller meets. My good friend Victor almost always won the 100-meter hurdles. The season was enjoyable and I was getting to spend time with friends. From a competitive standpoint, I was average and was not necessarily highly focused on winning like I was in my other sports.

One day about three weeks before the regional meet, the state qualifying meet for seventh and eighth grades, I happened to get to practice a little late because I was making up a test. As I came out of the locker room a couple of the high jumpers were in the gym practicing, including my good friends who were on the seventh grade team and a couple high jumpers from the girl's team. I was giving them a hard time, and an eighth grade female high jumper, Lashonda McMath, said "T.J. why don't you give it a try." So I did, and the first time I landed on the triangle metal bar. Lashonda gave me a few pointers and demonstrated for me. My good friend, Carlos Kincaid, also took a couple of jumps and then I decided for fun that I would go again. This time clearing the bar. Then I would go again and clear it, but the bar was not very high. It was definitely under 5'0".

Later that week, Coach Howard said that in the next meet we could pick one event to do or try. The meet was in Taylorville, Illinois and was only a dual meet. I asked to compete in the high jump. I thought it would be fun. Coach tried to talk me out of it as he said we had two guys that could clear heights that would most likely place them at the IESA state meet. I wasn't focused on the state meet; I just wanted to do it for fun. Coach said ok as long as I ran the hurdles and then I could high jump. I did not long jump in that meet. I started at the opening height and continued to clear the bar. Eventually, winning the high jump competition and clearing 5'4". I beat the other two high jumpers from my team. In the hurdles, I took third and one of my fellow teammates who was trying the event beat me, which ended my hurdling career.

The next week, we had a city-wide track meet with the three middle schools. Before the meet started, a freshman high jumper named James Ballard was finishing up a workout. James went on to become a junior college national high jump champion, competed for the University of Arkansas where he became an All-American, and competed at the US Olympic trials. As I was warming up he gave me a few pointers. I went on to win the city meet and cleared 5'4" for the second time in two weeks.

The next week was the regional meet, the qualifier for the IESA state meet. This was the biggest meet of the year so far and we were hosting it at our high school football stadium and track. I would go on to win the high jump and tie the seventh grade large school state record of 5'6". The next week was the Illinois IESA State Meet. I would go on to win the seventh grade state high jump title in a jump off with John Cliff from Decatur, Illinois. He would later go on to play NCAA Division 1 basketball at Marquette University. I also cleared 5'8" in the jump off to break the seventh grade large school state high jump record.

Over the summer, I played baseball in the Fairview Park Sandy Koufax League. At the end of the season I was picked up by one of the teams that qualified for the Sandy Koufax state tournament to play with them in the tournament. On my down time over the

CHAPTER 3

T.J. Jumper after winning the 8th Grade IESA State Basketball tournament

summer, I would go swimming or work on my basketball skills. I also attended basketball open gyms at Lanphier High School. Going into the eighth grade, much was the same as seventh grade. My grades were good, I played recreation soccer in the fall, and I played basketball in the winter. Our eighth grade basketball team started to develop quite the reputation and expectations. Leonard Walker moved into our school boundaries and joined our basketball team for eighth grade. He would go on to play NCAA Division 1 basketball at the University of Illinois-Chicago. The team had three guys close to 6'0" or taller with Victor being the tallest at 6'4". All three of those guys could dunk and would dunk during games. I could grab the rim one-handed and started to try to dunk a tiny basketball. By the end of basketball season I was close to 5'8" and could grab the rim with two hands. For home games, the stands would be packed with people wanting to watch us play. All the high school coaches in the city would come regularly to watch us as well. By the end of the season, we were undefeated and won the eighth grade IESA large school state basketball tournament.

As most of us moved into track season, we talked about adding one more team trophy to the school's trophy case, and we were referring to a team state track title. What I didn't know was that coach was not only going to have me do the high jump, but also run the 800-meter run. I reluctantly did so. I would get one to two jumps in at a meet and then I would have to go run the 800. Then, I would go back and finish high jumping with extremely dead legs. I only remember clearing 6'0" once before the city track meet because I always had heavy legs from training for and racing the 800. I decided to just run alongside my good friend Tim for most of the season if we were in the 800 together. One

CHAPTER 3

meet in Decatur, I felt physically fresher than I did in previous 800 races so my competitive spirit took over and I ran a low 2:20. Then, I started running it faster and faster and started to win some races.

At the regional track meet, the qualifying meet for the IESA State Meet, I was able to complete the high jump before the 800 meter run started. I won the regional and cleared 6'2". Later on in the meet I ran the 800 against the prior year's 800-meter seventh grade champion. After the first lap I took the lead. Shortly after the former state champ passed me. I ran a 2:12, finished in second place, and qualified for state.

The IESA State Meet was a little chilly with bouts of showers. I was scheduled to compete in the high jump and the 800, both on Saturday. The high jump came first and all of a sudden the first call was made for the 800. The only problem was that there were only two other competitors beside myself left in the high jump competition. I hated running the 800 so I begged my coach to let me scratch out of it and finish the high jump competition. He told me that since I was going to finish in the top two he would let me scratch the 800 meters. I went on to win the eighth grade state large school high jump title and tied the state record by clearing 6'2". As a team we also went on to win the team title that year as well.

The summer after eighth grade was spent playing in basketball open gyms, swimming, camping, and playing baseball. The baseball season went great. My team did not finish in the top two, but I was picked up again by a team to play with them in the Sandy Koufax State Tournament as a pitcher, catcher and infielder. As a team, we made it to the semifinal game against the number one seeded team. In the third inning I was playing as a catcher when a bang-bang play occurred in which a player on third tried to steal home as the pitcher received the ball back from me. The pitcher started to walk back to the mound with his head down, so the runner took off. The pitcher threw me the ball once he noticed the runner trying to steal home. I blocked home plate with both knees down and one of the runner's metal cleats slid up my thigh. I held onto the ball, the player was out, and the umpire immediately called time because of the cut on my pants and the blood gushing out. My baseball season was over along with the rest of my summer activities when I was taken to the hospital and received fifty-seven stitches in my thigh. As I was healing at home, I realized that as a ninth grader I was going to have to make a decision as to which sport I would compete in because the high school baseball and track season were both during the spring season.

Lessons learned

1. I knew I loved competing and enjoyed the sports that I played.
2. Decided what I wanted to do in the future was to win a state title and earn an athletic scholarship. I was confident that I had what it took.
3. Learned I may have a gift that I didn't know that I had, high jumping.
4. The decision to play baseball or run track was a difficult one for me. It was the first time in my life that I would have to make what I thought was a tough decision. How would this go? What if I made the wrong decision?
5. I had to cope with my first major injury and not being active playing sports. I had to push through the mental

and emotional side. I learned a lot about myself.

Reader self-reflection

1. What gifts do you have? How do you use your gifts?
2. How do you overcome tough situations?
3. Who are people you could turn to for guidance and support?

Chapter 4

Ninth Grade

The decision of what high school to attend was not as cut and dry as some would believe. As a family there was a little debate as to whether I should go to Sacred Heart-Griffin (private catholic school), Mt. Pulaski where my dad taught and coached, or Lanphier High School (feeder public school of my middle school). Lanphier had a bad reputation as an inner city school with a lot of discipline issues and fights. But, ultimately it was an easy decision as the older neighborhood boys (JP and Tim) attended and gave great feedback about the school and the teachers. Also, there was going to be talent in all four sports I was considering and the coaches were known to be outstanding. The other two schools we were considering had great academic reputations, but there were questions regarding the quality of at least one of the sports I was considering and the school's facilities for that sport. Those two schools were considered elite in at least one of the sports, but when all four sports were viewed as a whole, Lanphier had the most to offer athletically for me and would offer a quality education as well.

The soccer team at Lanphier struggled with wins, but I knew

CHAPTER 4

a bunch of players on the team. The varsity basketball coach, Coach Nika, was a legend and in the Basketball Hall of Fame. I had also attended many open gyms. The team's record over the last couple of years had struggled, but the program had a strong following from the 1980's. The two spring sports (track and baseball) both had very good coaches, and had very good programs.

Although there were times that Lanphier's reputation was fulfilled, the majority of the days it was not. I always felt safe, had great support, supportive teachers, and amazing administrators. In Illinois, the boys high school soccer season was a fall sport, so practice started early in August and I was able to get to know my teammates before school even started. Coach Phillips, my new soccer coach, was known to get the best out of the players he had as many did not have a competitive soccer background. He also was known to have a team that was always in shape. The first week of soccer practice was tough as it was the hardest conditioning I had done. I was sore all over, and one morning I even threw up at the end of conditioning. We typically did two-a-days until school started. I was fortunate enough to start varsity soccer as a freshman. Throughout the season, there were growing pains, but Coach Phillips regularly challenged me.

One day in the fall, my friend Victor and I were sitting in the gym for PE class. The track coach Mr. Garcia was our PE teacher. He said to us that we would one day be state champions. We thought he was talking about basketball as the community had already put expectations on our class for basketball because of how well we did in middle school. However, he would later tell us he was talking about track.

As the fall ended, preparations for the basketball season began.

The very first practice Coach Nika called four of the freshmen (Victor, Jeff, Leonard, and me) into the locker room and asked us how we felt about playing varsity basketball. He also talked to us about how to handle playing varsity as it would not always be easy and some of our teammates might be unhappy. Victor and I started the very first game of the season. By winter break, Jeff and Leanard would join us and a sophomore in the starting line-up. Although we had a losing record, we had doubled the number of wins the team had the year previous, and we had upset some teams that were ranked in the state.

As basketball season came to an end, a big decision was heavily weighing on me. I had to decide what I was going to do about baseball and track in the spring. My parents and I talked about trying to do both sports, but knew it was going to be extremely difficult. We had conversations with the athletic director, baseball coach, and Coach Garcia, the track coach. He said there was a really good chance that I could high jump on the varsity team. There were multiple conversations with my parents about the pros and cons as to which sport to choose. Eventually, I had a conversation with Coach Garcia because I had one major concern with track, running the 800. In a very freshman way, I mentioned that I would play baseball if I had to run the 800. Coach Garcia decided to make me a deal. If I cleared 6'4" in my first meet, I would not have to run the 800 in my high school career.

The deal sealed my decision. My biggest concern about not competing in track was not knowing how high I could go in the high jump. If I really missed baseball, I could have played in one of the summer leagues. Fortunately, I fell in love with high jumping as it was me vs. myself. And nothing could compare to the feeling of flying over the high jump bar. In short, I did not miss baseball as much as I thought I would. Although I did follow the team's success as I knew most of the guys on the team.

The first couple of weeks of practice started for indoor track. At the end of the first week, Coach Garcia had the high jumpers engage in a jump off in the old gym off of the wood gym floor. There were three of us in the jump off. Rudy was a junior, and Victor and I were freshmen. I won the jump off so I won the opportunity to compete at the first indoor meet at Western Illinois University's High School Meet. The next weekend we headed to the first meet. The high jump competition was on the gym floor at Western so I had to wear running shoes.

I really did not know what I was doing. I did not have set measurements for approach steps, but I did run back from the bar and count my steps. Once I counted to ten right steps (every time my right foot touched down) running a reverse "J", I would put a piece of tape down for my run-up starting point. I started at opening height, and made it to 6'0" with only a couple of competitors left. At 6'2", there was only one other competitor and I left. We both cleared 6'2" and the bar moved to 6'4". This was a big attempt for me as I did not want to have the possibility of running the 800 in high school. The other jumper cleared the hight on his second attempt, and I missed on my first two attempts. On the third attempt, I cleared the bar and set a new personal record (PR). The other competitor and I both missed at 6'5". However, because he cleared the prior height on his second attempt and I cleared it on my third attempt I ended up in second place. This scored eight points towards the team race. My teammates who were mainly upperclassmen for this meet were very complimentary and supportive.

The rest of the indoor season we had a couple more meets.

Some of the big meets were at Eastern Illinois University and at Oak Park-River Forest High School. The one thing I discovered pretty quickly with the upperclassmen was the history of Lanphier track and field and the pride that the team had for competing and winning. Our sweats we used for warm-ups even had "north side pride" on them. This was definitely the culture of the team. You work hard and you compete with pride. It was like all the former Lion track athletes were with you.

Throughout the rest of my freshman year, the focus was on learning technique and the event of the high jump. One of the first things Coach Garcia did as soon as we could get outside on the track was to have me run back my approach from the bar and he counted my steps. He had me stretch out my arm and put my wrist on the first tape mark on the bar, and then run a reverse J. After putting steps down, I now had a consistent starting spot. We measured out my approach and I would use those measurements every time coach had me work on my approach in practice and when I competed in meets. Approach work usually occurred twice a week and for outdoor season, we typically had two to three meets a week as coach had me jump in freshman, sophomore, and varsity meets. In the lower level meets, I would sprint on a relay and also long jump. We had plenty of sprinters, so I usually did not do any open events unless coach wanted me to run the 100 meters or the 200 meters for some short sprint conditioning or curve work.

On a regular basis, my coach would give me articles or handouts about high jumping techniques. He even gave me a small paperback book written by a college coach on technique. About once a week during the outdoor season, coach would have me watch videos with him to look at professional high jumpers and also review tapes of my own jumps in meets. One time coach told me that if I wanted to be one of the best I had to become an expert in my event. Coach gave me every opportunity to do that with these sessions. Rudy the other varsity high jumper would join us and we would watch his jumps as well. These high jump learning sessions required one to two hours outside of practice a week.

Towards the end of the outdoor season, I was able to place top three at the city meet and conference meet. Fortunately, the two high jumpers (Charles and James) who placed ahead of me were upperclassmen from a different high school, but they were also supportive. James Ballard was one of the guys who helped introduce me to high jump when I was in junior high, but he was not a high school teammate as he transferred schools. The sectional meet was after the conference meet and to qualify for state an athlete had to meet the qualifying standard or place in the top two in the event. The qualifying standard for the high jump was 6'6" and I had only jumped that once and that was at the conference meet.

The meet was at East St. Louis High School and the high jump field included three guys who had cleared the qualifying standard beside myself. Saying I was nervous would be an understatement. We laughed pulling up to the East St. Louis stadium because a sign said something like "no guns, knives, or automatic weapons allowed in the stadium." Also, East St. Louis was known to have a history of amazing track athletes. During the competition, I felt like I had heavy legs and would only clear 6'5" and miss at the state qualifying 6'6". James, Charles, and a high jumper from East St. Louis qualified for the Illinois State class AA (large school) high jump competition. I was extremely disappointed in my performance and that I did not qualify. I believe I was mentally overwhelmed by the environment, the intensity of the meet, and the high level of competition.

What I didn't know was that not qualifying would be a motivator and the turning point in building my confidence and getting me to focus on becoming a highly successful high jumper later on in my career. On the way home on the bus from sectionals, Coach Garcia called me up to the front of the bus and told me I was practicing tomorrow and competing on Monday. He also said that I was going to train all week as if I had qualified for the state meet and then I was going to the state to watch my teammates as well as get a feel for the meet. I was very grateful to get to go.

The Monday meet was the "Capital Area Classic," a meet for high school athletes in the area irrespective of the size of their school. You could compete in it if you were one of the top fifteen entries in field events and top eight entries in running events. If you qualified for state, Coach Garcia did not enter you in the Monday meet because he wanted your focus on the state meet and did not want you to get hurt.

Over the weekend I was bummed that I was competing on Monday as I felt it was a consolation for not making it to state. As I was pouting around over the weekend about not qualifying for state and competing at the Monday meet, my dad reminded me I was only a freshman. He also encouraged me to just have fun on Monday and to compete against myself. I decided to just go jump. I didn't pay attention to the other competitors. I distracted myself by talking with people in between jumps, running curves, or doing small skips to stay loose. This was the most relaxed I competed all season. I won the competition and cleared a new personal record (PR) of 6'7".

On Thursday, the team and I left for Charleston, Illinois where the state meet was being held. The team had two guys in the

400 meter dash (George and Andre), an athlete in the 300 meter hurdles (Jimmy) and one of the top times in the 4x400 meter relay. Upon arrival at the state meet track, coach had me warm-up, do a few approaches, and take a few jumps. It was all about me having some taste of the state track meet. We stayed in the dorms on the Eastern Illinois University campus and would walk to the track. Friday was all about qualifying for finals which would occur Saturday. Coach made sure I knew that the first flight on Friday set the qualifying height for Saturday's finals. When twelve or less competitors were left in the top flight, that was the height that determined finals qualification for the other flights. I actively watched the high jump competition and was upset when I saw competitors I had beaten earlier in the year were competing at state. But they came out of a different sectional track meet.

Even though there were a couple lows, most of my freshman track season was a huge positive. Although it was the one sport that I had the least experience in, it became one of my top two sports. I decided that I would not play summer baseball as I was not missing it, and I wanted to do more with track and field. I spent most of the summer playing basketball and also training and competing with a track and field club called the Springfield Striders. The Springfield Striders had most of the top track and field athletes from the city and a few from the surrounding area. I would also do workouts at my home track if it was open.

As a track club, we competed in the USA Track and Field (USATF) Junior Olympic meets. I ended up qualifying for the USATF Junior Olympic Nationals at Louisiana State University (LSU). This would be my first national-level meet and I had no idea what it would be like. We spent several days at LSU; the facilities were amazing.

T.J. at a Strider's summer track and field meet

My parents talked with me about just going out and doing the best I could. I decided I would just jump and have fun. The competition was during the evening session and the weather was in the nineties.

Coaches and parents could not be in the warm-up area or on the track. My dad walked me to the check-in area and then wished me luck. I would not be physically close to them for four hours. The high jump pit (that area where the high jump is competed along with the high jump mats) was located in the center infield of the track. Coach McBride (Southeast High School girls track coach at the time) and coach of the Springfield Striders held onto a light pole to see over the fence and to give me corrections. My family was watching from the top of a walking area attached to a building next to the track. After the three-hour competition, I tied my PR at 6'7" and was an All-American by placing seventh. This was the second meet that I competed relaxed, having fun, with no expectations, which allowed me the mentality of just doing the best I could. I had to learn to compete my best at the biggest competitions. I had to figure out what would work for me. Over the next three months (end of May through July) I learned what would work for me by competing in these meets. I was fortunate because some people have to wait until the next season.

Lessons learned

1. Had to make a major decision and had to work through a process to do that. This resulted in choosing track and field. I developed pros and cons, collaborated with those who I thought highly of, and asked questions to get information.
2. Learned how to overcome failure and how to persevere past it.
3. Learned how to compete with the best mind frame for me in order to do my best in the biggest competitions.

Reader self-reflection

1. How do you make a decision? What is your process?
2. Who can you bounce ideas off of to make the best decision? Are they similar to who you named in chapter 2 and 3? why or why not?
3. When have you done your absolute best? Are there certain routines, or mind frames that allowed you to do your best?
4. What steps could you take to get into that mind frame?

Chapter 5

Tenth Grade

Coming out of a successful summer, I was looking forward to my sophomore year. The fall soccer season was one that was up and down as I played a new position. The basketball season was up and down as well. We had a new coach, and I lost my starting position for about the first ten games of the year. After all of the struggles in the team sports, I was looking forward to track season. As soon as basketball season ended, I moved into track season. One of the things we discovered was that basketball was a great high jump trainer. I typically PRed or tied my PR within two weeks of the basketball season being over.

The indoor track season was similar to my freshman year. We went to many of the same indoor meets and I jumped at all of them once basketball season was over. The indoor season would be my coming of age and started to show that I could compete with the top high jumpers in the state. I would place in the top three in all the indoor meets at the varsity level. The biggest meet in which I made a name for myself was at Oak Park-River Forest. The top two high jumpers from the state meet the year before were seniors and competing at the meet. One of them did not know who I was before the meet began and saw me at the entry board looking at the order in which we jumped. The person who came into the meet with the highest reported jump was usually the last jumper at a height. I was third to last with the other two high jumpers jumping after me. This one competitor looked at me and said, "Are you scared to compete against us?" All he knew was that I was in the high jump competition, but he did not know who I was. I knew who he was, but I said, "No, I jump right in front of you" and I walked away.

After clearing 6'4", he looked at me and said "you good, you got hops." There was a lot of attention on the high jump competition as the state champ and the state runner up were in the competition and were both 7'0" high jumpers. There were about ten teams in the competition and if someone was not competing they were standing around the high jump competition to watch. The bar was moved to 6'6" and my two competitors started a clap for me and the crowd joined in. My excitement and adrenaline started to kick in while at the same time I was just focused on myself. I approached the bar and cleared it easily. Cheers from the crowd followed, and my two competitors congratulated me. They followed by jumping with a clap and clearing the height as well.

The meet had come to a standstill and all eyes were on the competition because not many regular high school meets had three guys jumping at 6'8" without any previous misses. I was the first jumper to be up at the height. A clearance would mean a new PR for me. I am really amped as the bar is raised to the 6'8" measurement. As I approached my starting mark (tape mark) to start my approach, the crowd started the clap again. It didn't matter what team anyone was on, everybody was clapping for all three of us. I approached the bar with a spring, took off, and hit the bar with my right shoulder on the way up.

Coach Garcia calls me over and tells me to back up the start of my approach about two inches. I frowned at him, and he said that "all high jumpers have a height when they have to start moving back a little from their starting mark in order to take off a little further from the bar so they have more time to get to their vertical height to clear the bar." I gave a nod and he then said, "Don't worry you will make the pit, just trust me." I did. I moved back from my starting mark about two inches. The crowd started clapping again. I took off on a sprint, jumped, and cleared the bar. After landing, I let out an emotional yell and the crowd cheered. I now had a new PR. Of the other two high jumpers, one cleared it on his first attempt (he was the former state champ), and the other cleared 6'8" on his third attempt.

Since there were still three high jumpers left, the bar was moved to 6'10". The crowd followed with their rhythm clapping for each jumper. I ended up missing all three jumps, and the jumper who missed twice at 6'8" also missed all three attempts at 6'10". The previous year's state champ cleared it and then cleared 7'0". I finished in second place and finished higher than the one competitor who was runner up at state the year before. Once the high jump competition concluded, the three of us gathered, talked a little, and then wished each other luck. There was a bond formed between us. Other athletes and coaches came up to us complimenting us as we walked to our separate team camps. I felt I had arrived and my confidence was at an all time high as I held my own with two future NCAA division 1 high jumpers. The former state champ was interviewed by a newspaper sports reporter and he mentioned my name as an up-and-comer in the event to watch out for.

CHAPTER 5

T.J. clearing a high jump bar at an indoor track and field meet

The next meet was the Illinois Top Times Indoor Meet where individuals were offered invites to compete if their event performance was good enough to be in the top twelve for the field events. I would place in this meet with some of the best high jumpers in class AA. Not all of them attended the meet, but the majority of them did. Jumping well in these big indoor meets, I applied the same mind frame of focusing on myself, competing against myself and the bar, and controlling what I could control. I consistently competed at a high level. I had learned and applied what I needed to do to be mentally and emotionally ready to compete at my best. I also learned from the previous year that if I did not make these preparations that it was all on me if my performance was not as good as I wanted.

During my ninth-grade season, the focus was learning basic high jump technique, whereas the 10th grade season focused on more specific techniques to jump higher. Coach Garcia discussed lengthening my high jump approach to get a little more speed. The other focus was increasing my physical conditioning reps, increasing the physical preparation. The first few weeks of the outdoor season did not go as planned. As soon as we could get outside for practice, coach worked on adding two steps to my approach. Over the next two weeks, I won meets but struggled with my approach and the heights I was jumping. I was struggling to clear 6'4" and 6'5", which was at least three inches lower than what I had jumped indoors.

This two-week period of struggle with my approach, stutter stepping and steps being off, was one of getting great support from my teammates and coaches. They would constantly give me words of encouragement at meets. Coach Jon, Coach Tony, Coach Caton, Coach Altmix, and Coach Cason were always there for me and supportive. At the time, I did not realize how lucky I was to have the coaches and teammates that I had at Lanphier. They were always protective of me and always pushed me in a positive way to reach my potential. The turning point of my approach struggle came in a Quincy High School junior varsity meet. Coach Garcia stayed at school to work with the upperclassmen at practice. The other coaches took the freshman and sophomores, including me, to the Quincy meet. I won the high jump competition but struggled with my approach really badly, even scratching one jump. Coach Cason was cheering me on during the competition, and then walked with me down to the long jump competition where I was jumping to try to help the team score points. Coach Cason said, "I don't know high jump technique but you are not smooth running up to the bar. I know you are better than that. We need to get this figured out, but you competed and got the job done. Now, go get some points in the long jump." We got back late. The next day Cason told Coach Garcia how everything went.

The day after was a recovery day as we had a home track meet the following day. Before I left practice, Coach Garcia told me he would watch how things went at the home meet with my approach. At the meet, I won the event, but struggled with my approach again. After the competition, Coach Garcia called my dad over to the high jump pit. Coach told me to stay on the high jump pit with my spikes on because we were going to figure out what was not working. Coach had me take another jump. Then he shouted, "I got it." When we lengthened to the new approach we forgot to include my three walking steps into the approach. Once we added those three steps in and started running from the longer approach mark, my steps were right on. He had me take seven approach runs and then had me jump at 6'4" and 6'6" a couple of times. That resulted in easy clearances and the smooth run back. Teammates hollered at me about how good it looked and the assistant coaches pumped their fists at me. Coach Cason came over in between running events and said, "He's baaaaack" and gave me a half-hug.

The rest of the season went like the indoor season. I was winning most varsity meets with jumps of 6'7" and 6'8" until the city and conference meets. During this time, it was also the hardest I had trained with stadium steps, plyometrics, and sprinting as well as working in technical work. The hardest training peaked between eight and ten weeks from the state meet. Then coach gradually backed the training down each week. As we were going week to week, Coach Garcia explained to me about how he was putting me through a peak cycle so I would physically be at my best for the state meet. This message was a positive way for me to know the expectations but also the confidence he had in me.

The city of Springfield had three high jumpers that had cleared 6'8" or higher. Seniors James and Chuck were at Southeast High School and were top eight placers the year before when I was a sophomore at Lanphier. We had a great relationship and continually supported each other even when we competed against each other. For the city schools, the city and conference meets were huge meets for teams. Lanphier, my school, was multi-time city track meet champions in a row (in the long run it ended up being at least twenty years in a row). As a team, we were also favored to win the conference title. In those competitions, I finished third behind James and Chuck, but jumped well.

The Friday after the conference meet was the sectional meet at Collinsville High School. The high jump competition was a tightly contested event as five guys would end up clearing the state meet qualifying mark of 6'5" and four of those guys would go on and place in the top ten at the state meet. This time I was not nervous and had learned from the big meets I jumped in over the summer and during the school year of how to compete at my best. I didn't watch the others jump. Rather, I focused on myself by distracting myself by talking with teammates, friends, competitors, and my parents. I ended up taking third by clearing 6'8" and finished behind Chuck and James. As a team we would go on to win the sectional title as well.

On the Thursday before the state meet the state qualifiers left school around noon and drove to Eastern Illinois University in Charleston to check into the dorms and practice on the track. The track was packed and coach told us to be safe. Coach Garcia had me take about seven approaches on the high jump pit and took about three jumps total at 6'2" and 6'4". He just wanted me to feel the track surface before the next day's competition.

CHAPTER 5

After having breakfast that Friday morning and laying around the dorms until mid-morning, we headed to the indoor track which was right next to the outdoor track. As soon as we got to the track, Coach Garcia went with me to measure out the steps for my approach. As a team we then hung out in the indoor track until it was time for each of us to warm up for our events. I was in the first flight (top flight) for the Class AA (large school) high jump competition. This flight would set the height that would need to be cleared by individuals in the rest of the flights to qualify for finals.

After warming up, I headed to the field event check-in gate. The main stands were on the opposite side of the track and the fence attached to the field near the check-in gate had a tarp on it so you could not see through it. As I approached the gate, an official opened it for me. As the gate swung open, I was overwhelmed with how big the crowd was and how loud the crowd was. My adrenaline kicked in, my heart started to pound, and my legs started to tingle. This was only the second time I had competed in front of a crowd that large (the other time was when I was at LSU), but the difference was the emotional intensity of the meet. You could just feel it in the air. I can still see that view and remember that feeling to this day when I think about it.

I took a few approaches and a couple of jumps to finish my warm-up. Everything felt good technically, but I still was overcome with the adrenaline and emotion of the moment. Everything was new from there forward because I had not competed at state as a freshman. Coach Garcia and I decided to take my first jump at the opening height of 5'10". This was a great decision as I still had tingling legs. As the competition started, my name was called. I approached the mark, tried to calm down and then took off in a sprint towards the bar and jumped. Unfortunately, I hit the bar on the way up and missed. As I stepped off the mat, I could see the worried look on my parents' faces, but they yelled "You got this." I got back to where my sweatpants were and Coach Garcia was standing outside the fence on the track curve peeking through bushes. He called me over and said, "Now that you got that out of the way, now we can compete." I started laughing because I had not missed at 5'10" since eighth grade.

The high jump official was using a competition format of five-alive so I waited a short period of time, seemed like less than five minutes before my name was called to be in the hole (third person) to jump. Most of the top high jumpers were not jumping at the opening height. They were waiting until higher heights to start their competition. A few of those ahead of me missed their second attempt. I had calmed and was now in the competitive mindset that I had used at other big meets during the year. I went up to my starting mark, started my routine of touching my toes and visualizing, then took off in a sprint, jumped and easily cleared the bar. Now I was ready to jump and compete.

The bar was raised two inches after all the competitors either cleared the bar or missed at a height three times and were out of the competition. The bar went to 6'0", 6'2", 6'4", and then a decision was made to go to 6'5" because there were close to twelve competitors left in the flight. Wherever the last bar cleared when the officials stopped the competition would set the height for the individuals for the other flights to clear. A couple of competitors missed on their third attempt so they were no longer in the competition, and the officials made the decision to move the bar to 6'6". I cleared it on my first attempt and so did most of the top ranked high jumpers. There were a couple of

CHAPTER 5

jumpers that went out so the qualifying competition was over. I had qualified for finals on Saturday which would be like a normal high jump competition and would decide the state champion and placers.

As a team we had several people in individual events and relays that had qualified for finals. The coaching staff took us out to eat for dinner and then back to the dorms for a short period of time. Since most of the team missed curfew the year before, the coaches decided to take us all to a movie. After the movie, we went back to the dorms for the rest of the night.

The next morning was the Saturday of state track finals. We ate breakfast and then had a team meeting. Coach Garcia would review each of our events and times along with the mind frame he wanted us to have. It became a tradition for Coach Jon to bring his state championship 4x100 relay medal that he won when he was in high school. We would rub it for good luck, and we always talked about how we wanted one of our own.

The temperature was in the nineties. We walked over to make camp in the indoor track. As the last few Class A (small school) high jump competitors finished, I started warming up with my sweats on and my rolled stocking cap. I started wearing my rolled stocking cap in cold weather at the eighth grade state competition. I continued to wear the stocking cap as a good luck omen and to keep everything a routine. It did matter what the weather was. If I was high jumping I had it on during warm-ups.

When the first call was made for the AA high jump competition I went to the field event check-in gate. This time when the gate opened I did not have the same feeling of adrenaline as I did the day prior. I was calm, but excited to compete. I was in the same mind frame I was in during the other big meets I had throughout the year. I was focused on me and doing the best I could. The high jump competition started at 5'11". I cleared each height on my first attempt. The jumps were 6'1", 6'3", 6'5", 6'7", and 6'8". Starting at 6'7", I moved my starting mark back two inches as Coach Garcia directed me as he stood behind the fence and in the bushes. At 6'8", he had me move back one inch. Then again at 6'9". After 6'7", the bars were moved up one inch at a time. Some of the better high jumpers passed on jumping until the bar was moved two inches.

At my first attempt at 6'9", I cleared it and set a new PR. Then I missed all three attempts at 6'10". I was also excited because I earned eighth place at state and I was also excited to watch the rest of the high jump competition because there were seven competitors left in the competition. By the end of the high jump competition, it would go down as the highest competition ever in state history. I was the last place winner and cleared 6'9", which would have won the event most years. The top five place winners all cleared 6'10" and the top three all cleared 7' 0" with the winner clearing 7'3". The state champion would also jump at the state record for the event, but would miss.

After the state meet, I was ultra confident and in love with high jumping. This would be when my mind frame changed from thinking I was going to play basketball in college to one of me thinking I could high jump in college. I was looking forward to the summer full of basketball and Junior Olympic track meets. My parents and I decided I would start a weight program, work out at my home track with Coach Garcia on open workout days, and basketball open gyms. Unfortunately, during the first part of June I seriously injured my back. I went to pickup a basketball at a morning workout and pulled a back muscle that was laying over one of my lungs. This ended most of my summer plans. Healing from this injury was a real struggle mentally and physically for me. It was extremely tough to take deep breaths.

After resting for about six weeks, we decided I would try to get back into training for the high jump. I took some jumps at lower heights and decided that I would try to qualify for Junior Olympics Nationals. At the meet, my back was doing fine until the competition started to get to about 6'6". When I tried to arch my back over the bar more, my back felt tight and like a pulling was occurring. I ended up clearing 6'7" and then dropped out of the competition. My parents and I decided I would be done for the summer and would allow my back to fully heal so that I would be ready for soccer season for the fall. Needless to say, all the excitement from the state track meet had worn off and the injury had me worried about getting back to where I was as an athlete.

Lessons learned

1. Failing and struggling can bring focus, growth, and improvement. Don't be afraid, take it head on. It is ok to be disappointed but you have to move forward and use it as a lesson learned instead of a negative. Make the most out of the situation.
2. In order to compete my best in the biggest moments, I could not compete angry or against others. I had to be focused on myself, be relaxed, and have fun. This put me in a mental place of being loose and very competitive (but not too competitive). This mentality allowed me to attack any situation with confidence and without fear.
3. Competing against a higher level of competition built confidence but also was a challenge that helped me improve. The national level competition helped put regular meets

and state level meets into perspective.

Reader self-reflection

1. How do you handle struggle/failure? Does the way you handle struggle/failure help you improve? Why/why not?
2. What might be ways you can improve your mental mind frame when struggling?
3. What is your mental and emotional state when competing? Does it allow you to do your best in the most intense moments or the biggest competitions? If not, what might you change to get to a better mental/emotional state while warming up and competing?
4. What level of competition would be just above the level you are currently playing?
5. How might an experience against one level higher improve you? The focus on the experience of playing at the higher level.
6. After playing at the higher level, what needs to improve?

Chapter 6

Eleventh Grade

After recovering from the back injury and getting back to a healthy state, I was looking forward to getting back in shape and ready for soccer season. The soccer season looked to be a positive one as we had many players back. The season started strong with lots of wins. As a team, we played in a mid-season tournament. In the semifinal game, I went for a head ball on a corner kick and took a knock to the head around the temple area. It swelled right away. I blacked out some, got to my feet, and waddled over to the bench. The referees stopped the game immediately, and I was helped to the bench. Then, I was sent to the hospital where tests showed I had swelling of the skull and a severe concussion. Over the next month, my normal day-to-day tasks were difficult. Right before the postseason, I was finally released to play again, but I was drastically out of playing shape. I typically viewed each sport as an off-season and preseason conditioning for the next sport. This was the first time I would head into basketball season not in maximum aerobic shape.

T.J. Jumper playing soccer for Lanphier H.S. as an 11th grader

I was hoping basketball season would be better than it was as a sophomore. There was a lot of attention around our basketball team because all of the starters were returning. Coming out of preseason, many high school basketball followers were aware of us as a team.

Early in the season, I would face a small setback. We were playing against Peoria Central when I went to guard a player on our press early in the first quarter. As he caught the ball, he took off. I planted my foot and went to change direction. Unfortunately, my foot slipped from underneath me. I heard a pop in my knee and felt sharp pain. This was the knee that I used as my high jump takeoff plant leg. I was helped off the court and was out the rest of the game. The Monday following I had a doctor's appointment for that injured knee and I was diagnosed with a strained knee ligament. I was fortunate as the ligament had been pulled and stretched, but because of my strength and flexibility of my stabilizer muscles the ligament did not tear. After a couple of weeks of physical therapy and treatment, I was back on the court full time.

The rest of the season went well until midway through the postseason. We won the first round championship which is called regionals. Four regions then come together to play a sectional tournament. The winner of the sectional would go to the supersectional which is the sweet sixteen in the state series. Many thought we would have a great opportunity to go to state, but we were upset in the first round of sectionals.

Although greatly disappointed in not going to state in basketball, I was excited for track season because I was the highest returning state placer in the high jump. Those who finished ahead of me at state and the two who finished after meet at the previous year's state meet had all graduated. The preseason outlook was that I could not only compete for a state title, but have a great chance to be a state champion. Others had recognized this as well, and it seemed to be the topic of conversation from teammates, coaches, competitors and friends.

The indoor track season went as expected as I won all the high jump competitions and even broke some meet records. Most meets I cleared 6'8" or 6'9". Going into the Illinois Prep Top Times Meet that was held at Illinois State University, I had the highest jump in Class AA in the state. Most of the high jumpers in the top fifteen would accept invites to the meet. The competition would reinforce the idea that I was the favorite for the state title. Throughout the competition, I was pretty clean clearing bars through 6'8". It ended up with another high jumper clearing 6

'8 " as well and we would have a jump off at 6' 10" for the meet title. I would end up clearing 6'10" to win the meet and earn another two inch PR.

Shortly after indoor season, Coach Garcia would have me enter into the tough portion of my peak cycle training. Again we would focus on the physical training piece and continue to work two-three days a week on technique. Now, we were focused on more finer details of technique. As the season progressed, I again was winning most meets. My confidence was at an all time high. We would use the home meets for technique as the track surface had aged, had cracks, and was worn down so much it was slippery even with spikes on. Fortunately, the school district would resurface the track after this season just before my senior year.

As I was training, I knew why behind what we were doing. I was no longer just doing what I was told and just getting it done. I was working and practicing with a purpose. About a month to three weeks before the sectional track meet, I would tie my PR as I again cleared 6'10" in Morton, Illinois at the Morton Relays. Then we followed those meets over the next couple of weeks at our home track with the city meet, which we won again and the conference meet. Since they were home meets I would usually start at about 6'2" and win at 6' 4". I then jumped and cleared 6'6" before calling it quits because of the track surface raising concerns about slipping and getting hurt. I jumped and cleared 6'6" because we knew that the state the qualifying height was usually 6'6".

My confidence remained at an all time high as each week I would check the Illinois Top Times publication to see if anyone was close with jumps from their meets. For most of the year, I was three to four inches higher than anyone else in the state. I

CHAPTER 6

went into meets confident I would win and really not thinking about it much as it was feeling easy. I would go jump and win with little push or competition.

The sectional meet was in Collinsville again and was like any other meet. The qualifying mark for state was 6'6". I hit that mark on my third total jump of the competition qualifying for state. All three were clearances. Only two of us would qualify as no one else cleared the qualifying mark. I jumped by myself for the rest of the competition as I was the only one left. I jumped at 6'8" and cleared it, I jumped at 6'10" and cleared that too. I had the bar set at 6'11" after talking with Coach Garcia. I cleared it and set a new PR. I then tried 7'0" and missed all three jumps, but had good attempts at it.

I was fired up for the state meet. When the flights and seeding came out, I had the highest jump by four inches. I thought it would be like any other meet where I would go compete, jump, and win. There was a lot of talk and attention on me being the favorite to win the state title. The week of practice was like the state week practice the year before. We would leave on Thursday to check into the dorm rooms at Eastern Illinois University and then have a light practice.

The first day competing was on Friday and served as the qualifying competition for finals, which would be held on Saturday. I was the last jumper in the first flight as I had the highest jump in the state from sectionals. As I warmed up, I was completely relaxed and loose as it was my second year competing at state. Plus, I was easily rated as the number one seed. I would end up passing at the opening height and only take three jumps to qualify for the finals. I felt good and confident going into finals the next day because I took the least amount of jumps compared to anyone in the competition.

I woke up the morning of the finals, had breakfast, and participated in our typical team meeting before heading over to the track. I was thinking that I was going to go over and get a state championship. My warm up went well. I felt good, but maybe I was too relaxed. Coach Garcia and I talked about me entering the competition at 6'2" or 6'4". We decided to wait until after warm ups. First call was made for Class AA high jumpers, so I headed to the field check in gate. I had my starting mark measured out, took a couple of approach runs, scissor jumped opening height during warm-ups, and then took another jump.

Coach Garcia and I then decided that although everything looked good and I felt good that it would be okay to just get into the competition instead of sitting around as I was already passing opening height and the bar that followed. All the other high jumpers entered the competition within the first or second height of the competition. Coach Garcia and I decided we would start at 6'2" to get a jump in, which is just when it started to look like a storm was coming. The 6'2" height was something I had cleared in every competition starting in ninth grade. As the high jump official started to get closer to my name, about five jumpers away, the storm unleashed a downpour of rain. It was hard to see. By the time the official got to my name, I was the only jumper left to jump at 6'2" as the others had cleared it or were out of the competition.

The change in weather and the pouring rain led to one of the toughest experiences of my life. The high jump officials decided that I must jump at the bar in this weather because I am the only jumper who has not jumped at the height of 6'2". Some of the other high jumpers cleared 6'2" when the sun still was out, and a couple of high jumpers jumped when it started to rain.

CHAPTER 6

As my name was called, I approached my mark. Between me and the bar, the track surface had large puddles of water on it. I could barely see the mat. I started my visualization process and started my run as I always did. I went to plant and jump and my foot slid out from under me as I took off. With all of the speed I had built up in my high jump approach, I slammed into the high jump mats and flipped head over feet across the top of it. Somehow the bar fell off as I was going underneath it. The top of the mats felt like a pool of water, and I was soaked. I was also mentally in disbelief of what just occurred. I was stunned.

The high jump official then told me I had to go again as I was still the only high jumper left at that height, but I had up to five minutes before having to take another jump. In the meantime, the running events were all postponed and called off the track. The high jumpers were the only ones out in the weather, and workers had to use a squeegee in front of the mat right where I just slipped and fell. Coach Garcia told me that I could do it. I thought that I was mentally ready to take my second attempt in the rain at 6'2". I followed my normal pre-jump routine, I took off sprinting into my approach, and went to jump. I slipped again and slid across the top of the high jump mat. I was again flying feet overhead under the bar. This time I felt a pop in my ankle and excruciating pain.

One of the meet officials who we saw at a lot of our home meets was working the runner's check-in tent and saw me slip in the pouring rain. He was not working the high jump competition, but he came out of the tent and yelled at the high jump official to halt the competition because of the bad weather. The head meet official intervened and told the check-in official to calm down. Fortunately, the competition was postponed. I asked to go see an athletic trainer as we wait for the weather to clear up.

The high jump official told me "no" and that I had to go with the other competitors to the tent. The check-in meet official yelled at the high jump official that he is taking me to the trainer whether he approved or not because he could see I was hurt and injured.

I was crying in the athletic training room as I was scared because of the pain in my take-off leg ankle. I was stunned because I had not missed at 6'2" in the last three years. It was usually my opening height. My sister came in tears to check on me and stayed with me. The athletic trainer said I had a severe sprained ankle that may also have a tear in it because of the pop that had occurred. He iced it for thirty minutes as it was still raining, then sprayed my ankle with something to ease the pain while I competed, and finally taped the ankle. My dad stopped in and encouraged me to battle through and just do the best I could. I could not walk let alone run without sharp pain. Coach Garcia told me it was up to me if I wanted to continue. The athletic trainer had me do some ankle movement tests. He said that he thought I could continue if I could handle the pain, and he think that with it taped up that I would do anything worse to it.

My dad and sister helped me walk over to the team camp that was in the indoor track facility. It was still pouring outside. My teammates came and checked on me. Coach Garcia asked what I was going to do. I said I was going to jump. Coach Garcia told me to warm back up as much as I could. We then heard that the field event competitions would be moved inside. I had about thirty minutes to warm up. My ankle was in severe pain. I took an approach and then I took one practice jump as all other competitors left in the competition were allowed to do. Coach Garcia reminded me that I had to clear the bar or I would end up getting last, thirteenth place, in the finals. My name was called for my third attempt at 6'2". I was nervous and sweating. My heart was pounding, and my legs were tingling and numb. I took my approach much slower than normal because of the pain and then jumped as hard as I could. I cleared it and gave a huge yell because of the relief, but also the pain.

Coach Garcia then approached me and said I was now in twelfth place and that I would have to jump at every bar to try to move up in place. There would be no passing of heights for the rest of the meet. Through pain, I jumped and cleared 6'4", 6'5", 6'6", and 6'7". I moved all the way up to fifth place before going out at 6'8". The state champion cleared 6'9" to win. I was devastated as I was the favorite in the event and finished fifth. Many people complimented me for pushing through the injury and battling back to place so high. My dad told me not to be too upset as I finished higher than I did before.

In an individual event, the results are all on yourself. The questions from those who were not at the meet like "what happened?" or did I "choke" burned. I didn't have an answer as I didn't want to give an excuse. Basically, I was not mentally prepared to compete in the rain and I had taken things for granted. I took the result so hard that I battled minor depression. I didn't want to talk with anyone. I didn't want to go out in public. I just wanted to stay in my room by myself. I was still dealing with the ankle injury, and had to stay off of it for a while, which made things even more difficult.

After I was released to jog or run in a straight line, my dad called Coach Garcia. The next Monday morning, Coach Garcia called at about 7 a.m. to tell me he would have the track open for me to do a running workout. He said it was time to get back at it and move forward. I went to the track and completed 10 x 100 meter sprints. The ankle was tight but not sore because the sprinting was just on the straight aways. After the workout, I was stretching and was all alone on the track as the distance runners went running off campus. As I sat there, I had a piece of mind and decided to let the anger and sadness go. It was a new day for me, and I decided to own what had happened. If people asked if I choked, I would answer "yes." If people asked what had happened, I would answer, "I wasn't mentally prepared." Those questions still burned, but I used them to push me to improve.

As the ankle started to heal, I got back into training for the high jump as I planned to compete in a few summer meets. I was invited to the National Scholastic Meet at North Carolina State University and Junior Nationals at Mt. Sac College in California. Besides the state meet, I had a really good season and met the qualifying standards for these national meets.

The National Scholastic Meet was basically the high school national meet. Both my parents flew with me to North Carolina for the meet. The first day of the meet was qualifying for finals, which I did fairly easily. The qualifying mark was 6'6 ¾". In the high jump finals, it was a who's who of the top high school high jumpers in the country. I had just finished my junior year of high school and some of the competitors had just graduated high school and would be college freshmen in the fall. This was the biggest meet I had ever competed in. Years later some of the track competitors would be Olympians and have sponsor contracts. I ended up taking fourth place by clearing 6'10 ¾". The winner was going to be a freshman in college in the fall and competing at the NCAA Division 1 level. He cleared 7'3" to break the meet record.

My confidence was back in a new and improved way because of how well I jumped. We flew back to Springfield and were home for a couple of weeks. I trained during that time. My dad and I then flew out to the USA Junior National meet at Mt. SAC College in Walnut, California. The Junior National meet was for U.S. citizens who were twenty years old or younger, and it was a part of the tryout process for the junior national team. What I didn't know at the time was that the meet would be extremely strict, even having random drug testing for place winners. Meet officials had to be with you if you went to the restroom during the competitions. I also did not realize that the meet would involve athletes who just completed their freshman year of college.

After warm-up, the high jump official called all the competitors together to review the event rules and tell us the order of jumpers. I was surprised to find out that I was the youngest competitor in the competition and that the open height would be at 6'6". When I looked around, there seemed to be athletes competing from some of the top NCAA Division 1 college track and field programs along with some of the better high school seniors in the country. There was even a competitor from Puerto Rico.

As warm ups were called to a halt, the bar was set to 6'6" for opening height, and since I was the youngest competitor I was first in the order. This was the highest I had ever started in a competition. I was a little overwhelmed with what was going on around me and with who I was competing against. As my name was called I approached my starting mark, took off sprinting, and clipped the bar on the way down. First jump and my first miss of the competition. My dad made a comment to me from behind the fence and I started laughing. This relaxed me and got me back into the mindset where I was just competing and focusing on myself. For my second attempt, I cleared the bar pretty easily. I would go on to finish in seventh place and then watch a future college competitor jump at 7'5".

The two meets were a great way to end my season and jump start me into my senior season. We decided to forgo the USA Junior Olympic National meet that I competed at after my freshman season because it had already been a long summer. There were also some soccer and basketball events that I had planned to play in. Plus, some college coaches started to get in contact with my dad and myself to talk about college track & field opportunities.

Lessons learned

1. Success is not a straight path. There are peaks and valleys. Valleys are where you learn and grow.
2. Success built my confidence, but I took it for granted and it took the edge off of my focus. I became lackadaisical mentally.
3. When you win, it is fine to be happy, but don't be satisfied until you achieve your goal.
4. I had to learn how to deal with disappointment and persevere.
5. The pain of disappointment reinvigorated me to work harder and be more focused on the "what" and "why." It also narrowed my focus and enhanced my desire to achieve my dream of being a state champion.

Reader self-reflection

1. How do you handle disappointment? Does the process you use allow for the disappointment to become a positive or does it drain your confidence?

2. Are you scared to fail or are you scared to make a mistake? If your answer is yes, you are holding yourself back from reaching your potential through learning.
3. What is your "why?" Why do you do what you do? What is your motivation (refer back to chap.1)? Will it pick you up and get you back to work when you're tired, sore, or had a bad result?

Chapter 7

Senior Year

After the disappointment of the state track meet, working through the disappointment, getting back to practice, and the success at the summer national meets, I vowed that everything I did would be connected to the state track meet in the spring. The way I trained for other sports, how I lived everyday with how I acted, and even when I decided to rest and relax to refocus all connected. I was "all in" on making sure I did the best I could at the state meet. The failure in my junior year, now looking back, resulted in many positives. Everything I did was purposeful while also balancing it with being happy. The other sports I played, my personal life, school, and my parents ensuring I had social time allowed me to live with a balance.

At the beginning of August, I set some personal goals of not only being a state champion, but also going to state or being named "All State" in my other two sports. Academically, I wanted to finish my high school career in the top fifteen GPA's in my class. I also had started the recruiting process and talking with some coaches. Although I knew I wanted to high jump in college, I also wanted to entertain all options with the other sports if I was recruited (which I was) to ensure I would make the best long-term decision for me. I received calls from multiple colleges from all across the country that started at the end of July and continued until I made my college decision.

The fall of my senior year involved school soccer. I wanted to be in the best shape I could be in and also serve as a leader on the team. I viewed soccer as my out of season base conditioning. Anytime we did conditioning, I used it as a competition. I wanted to either lead it to control the pace, or win at it if we were all going at the same time. There were not a ton of expectations on the team, but our coach was great at playing at a higher level than probably what we thought we could. By the end of the year, my team broke the school's win record. Individually, I broke the school's single season assist and scoring records, led the city and area in total offensive points, was named the conference soccer play of the year, and was named All State.

After soccer season I took a couple of college recruiting visits. For a brief time between basketball season and soccer season , I thought about not going out for basketball. In my high school career, some of my toughest moments were related to basketball and my role on the team. I felt like what I was asked to do and not do held me back as a player. But, more importantly, I wanted to focus so much on the high jump preparation and the recruiting process. After a back and forth conversation with my dad, I decided to play because I would have regretted not playing long after high school. I also knew it was one of the best ways to physically train for the high jump because of the running and jumping movements demanded in the game. I would also find time either dunking basketballs after practice or doing some high jump drills on the gym floor to continue working on preparing for the track season.

Going into the basketball season there were extremely high expectations for the team. Three of my fellow seniors were being recruited by NCAA Division 1 programs, and I was seeing some recruitment for soccer and a lot of recruitment for track. I would also have small recruitment opportunities for basketball, but it was widely known since I was ranked nationally that I would most likely go to college for track. During the season, our basketball team would emerge to a seventh ranking in the nation and number one in the state of Illinois. Then we would have some unfortunate losses and would drop a little in the polls. We were fortunate to play in some big time shoot-outs and tournaments that ranged from Pine Bluff, Arkansas, to Chicago to St. Louis. We would end up seeing some of the top high school basketball players in the country throughout the season.

As a team, we ended up winning our conference title, won the regional, won the sectional tournament in overtime, and then moved on to the super sectional also known as the sweet sixteen. We ran into a very tough Peoria Manual team that would eventually have multiple college basketball players and two Illinois Mr. Basketball players. We lost. The expectations, with that loss, were not met by the team and my basketball career was over.

After talking with Coach Garcia and my parents, we decided that I would take a full week off of all athletic training to relax mentally and physically from the long basketball season. Although mentally I wanted to get to training, the short time off allowed me to reset. That time also allowed me to announce my commitment to the University of Illinois and its track program. This allowed me to only have one focus and that was becoming a state champion.

I was already in good shape from soccer and the basketball

season. Coach Garcia decided that we would fully start my specific training the week after the Illinois Prep Top Times Meet in order to have a peak cycle around the sectional and state track meets. By the time basketball was over, there was only three indoor meets left. Therefore, we worked to maintain my physical shape and put focus on high jump technique. We started back at the basics and worked up over my first two weeks of practice. The weather was still cold, so as a team we worked on running in the hallways of the school and technique work, along with plyometrics, were in the gym. I did not jump for height or work on approaches in the gym. We just did drills and short jumped some.

At the end of the second week of practice, the team and I had two indoor meets over the weekend in the Chicago area. The first meet was Friday night in Proviso. We left mid-morning and made the approximate four-hour drive north. I waited to start the high jump competition at 6'0" because I had taken many jumps or approaches at practice. I was a little lethargic competing, but ended up clearing 6'6" to win over another high jumper because of less misses. The second meet was on Saturday at Oak Park-River Forest. I looked at these back-to-back meets in the first weekend as if I was competing to qualify one day and then competing for a title the second day. This was like it would be at the state track meet. Going into the Oak Park-River Forest meet, I was the favorite and received a lot of attention at the competition. I started at 6'2" and ended up getting first eventually clearing 6'11". For most of the higher heights I was jumping by myself as the only competitor left. I was satisfied because of how I performed on back-to-back days.

The next weekend was the Illinois Top Times Indoor Meet at the University of Illinois. I ended up winning the high jump competition and cleared 6'10". I had already signed a national letter of intent to attend the University of Illinois and compete in track and field. Mentally, I wanted to send a message throughout the state that I was ready to have a great season. This was the last indoor meet of the season and we would transition to the outdoor season. Every meet I had as a senior was focused on consistently going 6'10" or higher, but also jumping 7'0" or higher.

Over the next three weeks, Coach would put me through workouts to build strength. It was setting up the peak cycle. Coach let my parents know that it will be important for me to recover at night through eating properly and getting enough sleep as I would have tired and heavy legs from the workouts. One of the weeks was over spring break, and my family and I decided to stay home so I could train. My down time was hanging out with my girlfriend at the time, friends, and/or family. My entire focus was preparing to win state, so I very rarely stayed out late or did things that would physically hamper me. I stayed away from parties, drugs, and alcohol. This didn't hold me back from living, but it allowed me to justify to myself as to when it was time to go home. During workouts, the mentality of competing everyday at practice with myself pushed me to be better. There were multiple practices when coach had to tell me the workout was done and practice was over.

One great example of this was a stadium stair plyometric workout. In previous years, I would only do sets of five to six. As a senior with the increased intensity and competing with myself I would do sets of 8 on the stadium stairs. The other mindset change was related to weather. During previous years, my mindset would be "Oh it's raining, can we workout inside?" The same applied if it was cold. As a senior I wanted to practice in all kinds of weather because I wanted to be ready for state no matter what occurred. If it was raining pretty hard outside, coach had me high jump in practice and I looked forward to it to prove to myself that I could. I actually enjoyed it. The hardest practice was when I had a really bad sinus headache at a Saturday morning practice after a Friday night track meet. Coach had me jump for height and then take three jumps at each of the heights of 7'0" and 7'2". I didn't clear them, but he wanted me to work on my timing and seeing those heights so when I competed I had jumped at them before. Each landing with that sinus headache sent a throbbing through my head. This was the one time I complained to coach and he said, "What if you have a headache at State?" I shook my head and kept jumping until the workout was over.

Besides the one time I had a sinus headache, I looked forward to competing in all types of conditions. Those conditions could be wind, rain, cold, any combination of them, and sunny and hot. Throughout the season I won every high jump competition and cleared 6'10" or higher in every meet except for two. Consistency at going 6'10" or higher was a goal Coach Garcia and I had because even on a bad day a jump of 6' 10" could win state. The two meets I jumped lower than 6'10" occurred because I stopped jumping after winning the competition and clearing 6' 6". We pretended it was qualifying day at the state meet and I would be jumping for height the very next day as if it was state championship day.

Throughout the year, I was able to set multiple meet records and either break or tie my own school record. The last three weeks of the season were called the championship weeks for our team. Those three weeks consisted of the city meet, conference meet, sectional meet, and then the state meet. Our team had won multiple city meets in a row, and was thought to possibly win the conference and sectional meets and place at the state meet. I would go on to win the high jump competition at the city meet and conference meet. Although I won, I was not overly pleased with my performance at the conference meet because I felt like I had too many minor misses at lower heights. Although I would go on to win the meet and jump close to my personal best, I wanted more consistency as I did not want to leave the door open for other competitors at bigger meets.

The conference meet helped refocus me for the next week. The hard work and continually winning had me in a very confident mindset and not being happy after the conference meet put me in the mindset that I hadn't achieved anything yet. This is when I learned to be happy with performance, but not satisfied. Satisfaction would be winning the state title.

At the sectional meet, the qualifier for the state meet, I was ranked first and was the last jumper in the order. In order to qualify for state, I had to capture either first or second place or jump the qualifying height. The qualifying height for those competitors who finished third or lower was either 6'5" or 6'6". My focus was on winning the competition (qualifying) and then jumping high enough to be placed in the top flight at the state meet. Deep down I wanted to be the number one ranked jumper for the state meet. The weather at the sectional meet was hot and humid, but extremely windy. The wind was blowing in our faces as we approached the high jump mats. It was so windy that there were concerns from the meet officials that the bar would blow off for the high jump and pole vault competitions. Fortunately the bar would not be knocked down by the wind; the bar was knocked down only when it was hit.

I started the competition at 6'4" with most of the other

jumpers, except for two who were already out of the competition. I cleared my opening height on the first jump. One competitor went out so only two of us were left and qualified for state. The second place competitor went out at 6'6", and I cleared it on my first attempt. As the only competitor left, coach had me jump every two inches. Again, the focus was on jumping high enough to be in the top flight at state. I cleared 6'8" and 6'10" both on my first attempt at them. Then we decided to move the bar up one inch to 6'11". During my first attempt, I barely hit the bar with my ankles. So we made a minor adjustment and I had a huge clearance on my second attempt. My teammates had been watching and rhythmically clapping for each jump. Most of the other teams competing were watching now as well and joining in the clapping. We moved the bar to 7'0".

An announcement was made over the intercom that I was jumping at 7'0" and that I had broken the meet record. A clearance would be a new personal record for me in an official meet. First attempt, I cleared it and the stadium went nuts and my teammates and family were hugging me and congratulating me. After a couple of minutes, the high jump official came over to my coach and me to discuss he that they thought they missed measured. I would have to jump again and clear it. After some minor arguing between my coach and the high jump official, we decided to jump now at 7'1" instead of jumping again at 7'0". This decision meant I would not get the meet record, but our decision was to jump at a higher height so I would be ready for the state meet competition. I ended up missing all three attempts, but was happy that my performance was consistent, and did not have any misses until around my personal best. I felt ready for state.

The week of the state meet is when I was at the end of training and feeling my best because of the peak cycle coach had put me through. This is when my training load lightened up and I had more rest days. I had a lot of restless energy. The one negative in the week was when friends, teammates, classmates, and community members would wish me luck and also bring up my junior year. Things like, hope it goes better than last year or don't choke like you did last year. I continually would brush it aside, but it would burn my ego a little. I used the negative comments to remind me of my purpose. All the positive comments burned my fire and reinforced my motivation. On the Wednesday of the state meet, I went and got a massage to relax a little and make sure my body was primed for the weekend. During lunch on Thursday we left school to travel to Eastern Illinois University in Charleston for the Illinois State Track and Field Meet.

After checking into the dorms, we went to have a short practice at the track. It was packed with other athletes. Coach had me take a few approaches, a couple short 5-step jumps, and then two full jumps at about 6'4". Then, we went out to eat as a team followed by a little bit of free time. I was feeling restless during this time and worked to find a way to take my mind off the meet. A few teammates and I talked and played cards.

The next morning, we woke up and went to the dorm cafeteria for breakfast. I decided to not eat a heavy breakfast and stayed away from the pancakes and the biscuits and gravy. I went with cereal and an apple. With the focus on consistency, I wanted to be consistent with as much as possible, so I stuck to the routines I could maintain at the meet. The Class A (small schools) qualifying events went first. The Class AA (large schools) did not compete until the small school events were over. For the most part, our large school events started early in the afternoon.

CHAPTER 7

We left to walk to the track at about 10 a.m. I waited until the last Class A high jump flight had three athletes left and then I started warming up as I was the top ranked high jumper in the first flight (top flight) in the Class AA competition. I planned to have half my warm-up completed by the time I checked in because I had planned to pass at the first couple of heights until the bar reached 6'4". While the other jumpers were jumping at the lower heights I finished my warm-up. This allowed me to be ready to go for my first height instead of sitting around watching.

The qualifying competition started at 5'10" and would go up two inches at a time until there was anywhere from nine to twelve competitors left. The high jump official would make a final determination and that would set the qualifying bar for finals. I passed at 5'10", 6' 0", and 6'2" and took my first jump of the competition at 6'4". The high jump official thought that there were still too many competitors left so the bar was moved up to 6'5". I cleared it on the first attempt. The competition was halted after 6'5" and was set as the qualifying bar for the other flights. If a competitor cleared 6'5", he would qualify for finals the next day.

Emotionally, I was happy that I took minimal wear and tear because I only took two jumps to qualify for finals. I grabbed four bags of ice from the trainer and sat and watched my teammates compete as I iced my leg joints (ankles, knees, and hips). I wanted to ensure I was fully prepared for finals. The icing became a habit my senior year after competitions as a precautionary task. It put my mind at ease because I always felt fresher physically the next day than when I did not ice. I followed this icing practice after competing throughout the year, but especially if I would be jumping two days in a row. After my teammates competed, the assistant coaches (Coach Tony and Coach John) took me to get a sub sandwich as I was starving because I was competing over the lunch time and didn't get to eat. A few hours later, we went to eat at an all you can eat smorgasbord. Again, stuck to my usual type of dinner, followed by going to bed early.

The next morning, I followed the same pattern of eating breakfast and getting ready to go to the track. I wanted to keep everything routine. The one difference was that I took time to lay in my dorm room bed with my eyes closed and did some deep breathing to be as relaxed as possible. I told myself "I got this" and "it's just another track meet." The competition was not as big as the national meets I competed in the summer before. This was because of the caliber on the competition. The intensity and level of competition at nationals made it easier to handle the intensity and emotions of the state meet. We had a short team meeting and followed our tradition of Coach John showing us his state championship medal from the relay he ran on when he was in high school. Coach Garcia told us to just compete and that we were physically ready to go. Then we walked over to the track as a team and set up camp in the indoor track.

The weather was hot, humid, and sunny. The Class A high jump went first and my competition in class AA would follow. Occasionally I would walk out to see teammates compete or check-in on the Class A high jump. My parents, sister, and girlfriend came to see me in the indoor track to say hi and check in on me. Multiple family members including my grandma and a couple aunts and uncles came to the meet to watch me compete as well.

Once there were only three competitors left in the Class A high jump competition, I started warming up to have at least half of my warm-up completed before going out to the track. I waited for the final call to report. Since I knew the competition was going to start at 5'10", I would finish my warm up while the other competitors jumped at the lower heights. As I was finishing up warm up on the track, I heard my name called from behind me at the fence. It was my good friends Tim, Aaron, and Greg who came to cheer me on. It was amazing to have such support.

As the competition started, I passed at 5'10", 6'0", and 6'2". I entered the competition at 6'4". I cleared it on my first attempt. I didn't watch the other jumpers. Instead, I would talk to other competitors that I knew, talk with Coach Garcia, or with my friends behind the fence. The high jump officials decided to raise the bar one inch for the rest of the competition because of the number of competitors left. I passed 6'5" and waited to jump my second jump of the competition at 6'6". I cleared it on my first attempt. One of the other competitors who I thought was going to be my toughest competition missed all three attempts and was out of the competition. I became extremely relaxed, too relaxed after he went out. I thought my toughest competitors were out of the competition and that I had the title in the bag. This was almost a mental mistake on my part as I continued in the high jump competition.

I passed on 6'7" as the other competitors jumped waiting until 6'8". During my first attempt at 6'8", I hit the bar on the way up which resulted in my first miss of the competition. Coach told me to back up a couple inches from where I was starting my approach from. I took my second approach and hit the bar with one of my heels on the way down and knocked off the bar for my second miss. One more miss at 6'8" and I would be out of the competition. I would not have lived up to my ranking all year and the expectations I set for myself. This would have been failure two years in a row in my mind.

Coach Garcia called me over and told me I was not fully driving my knee and that I was being lazy at takeoff. This was not coach being difficult on me. It was our language for being in a better take off position. After reflecting back, I was too relaxed at the time because I was over confident of winning. After my name was called, I walked up to my starting mark, my legs were numb and the nerves had set in. I followed my normal preparation before each jump. I closed my eyes and did repeated toe touches as I visualized a great jump and clearance. My teammates, family, and friends started clapping in rhythm. I took off from my mark, jumped and had a massive clearance. As I landed, my emotions were at an all-time high as I was fired up. I stood up and let out a scream with a pump of the fist towards my family in the stands. My teammates and friends were cheering and shouting "You got this!"

With three people left in the competition, including me, I would be finishing in the top three. As I got back to talk to Coach Garcia, he said, "Now that is better...that jump is how you compete." He went on to advise me to jump at every height now. The next height was 6'9". One competitor went out, and the other missed at least once. I cleared it on my first attempt. Again, I pumped my fist and let out a yell upon landing on the mat and standing up. I was fired up and focused. The next height was 6'10" and there was only one other competitor left with me. I was in the lead because he had more misses. He was having a great competition as he had beat his personal best by a couple of inches. I cleared 6'10" on my first attempt and shouted again. I then went on and cleared 6'11" on my first attempt and was the only one left. I had become a state champion! I pumped my fist and yelled after every clearance from 6'8" and up. This was where my JUMP and SHOUT moment had finally occurred. I put everything into achieving a state title. I achieved a goal of earning a college scholarship and achieved a dream of being a state champion while also overcoming the failure at state the year before.

T.J. after winning the high jump state title and having his "Jump and Shout" moment

Lessons learned

1. If you want to be good, be a hard worker. If you want to achieve your "Jump and Shout" moment, compete with yourself in practice as if it was time for that moment.
2. Live as a champion in all parts of your life, live the right way and be respectful and humble. This includes resting when needed.

3. Surround yourself with people who support you. You will reflect the thoughts and actions of those around you. Appreciate the efforts of others.
4. State and national competitions are a roller coaster of emotion and momentum. As an athlete it is important to stay balanced so energy and emotion is not wasted. Don't get too relaxed or too excited.
5. There is nothing greater than achieving your "Jump and Shout" moment(s). The (s) behind moment was included because as I have gotten older I have learned that there can be more than just one of these moments in your life. Enjoy every minute of them.

Reader self-reflection

1. How do you practice? What would competing at practice look like for you? What should stay the same and what needs to change?
2. What does living like a champion look like in your life?
3. What areas of your life do you need to become an expert in?
4. How would you prepare mentally and emotionally for the roller coaster of emotions and momentum swings in high level competitions?
5. What are some techniques you can turn to in the moment to calm yourself down? Sometimes you need long-term preparation but also a quick fix depending on what the situation calls for.

II

Part Two

The foundation of what is needed to be highly successful and reach your goals and achieve your dreams. This section defines and elaborates on the four "Musts" and the characteristics needed for high success.

Chapter 8

Balance of the Four "Musts"

As a track and field Illinois state champion, I entered into a very small fraternity at the time. It had been close to forty years since the last male individual state track and field champion came from the city of Springfield. Since then, multiple other individuals have gone on to earn that title. I was positively overwhelmed by all the support and praise. I was fortunate to be recognized by the City Council and school board. Three or four signs entering Springfield from the highway were put up recognizing my name and achievement stating "Lanphier HS's T.J. Jumper 1996 Class AA High Jump State Champion." To this day one of those signs hangs outside my home high school track along with the school's other state champions and a picture of me hangs in the gym. I was also recognized as the State Journal-Register track and field athlete of the year.

This would not have been possible without all the support I had, including the coaching from Coach Garcia and the lessons learned throughout the years of competing. Having a growth mindset along with moving from being a hard working coachable athlete to one that competed against himself to be better allowed me to achieve my "*Jump and Shout*" moment of being a state champion.

> LANPHIER HIGH SCHOOL
> T J JUMPER
> 1996 IHSA CLASS AA
> HIGH JUMP
> STATE CHAMPION

Sign that was posted on the highway as vehicles entered Springfield, IL. Now hangs at Lanphier H.S.'s Memorial Stadium.

When I reflect on all the lessons learned, they all fall into one of four categories or what I call the four Musts: physical, technical, tactical and mental/emotional/social.

The <u>physical</u> refers to anything dealing with an athlete's body. The most obvious is the training one does during and outside of practice to prepare for competition. This refers to conditioning, fitness, weight training, speed agility, or anything else to improve athletic performance. The physical portion of training is usually the one area that coaches prepare for the athlete. What many miss in this category is the importance of nutrition and recovery. Both can prime the body for the athlete

Chapter 8

Balance of the Four "Musts"

As a track and field Illinois state champion, I entered into a very small fraternity at the time. It had been close to forty years since the last male individual state track and field champion came from the city of Springfield. Since then, multiple other individuals have gone on to earn that title. I was positively overwhelmed by all the support and praise. I was fortunate to be recognized by the City Council and school board. Three or four signs entering Springfield from the highway were put up recognizing my name and achievement stating "Lanphier HS's T.J. Jumper 1996 Class AA High Jump State Champion." To this day one of those signs hangs outside my home high school track along with the school's other state champions and a picture of me hangs in the gym. I was also recognized as the State Journal-Register track and field athlete of the year.

This would not have been possible without all the support I had, including the coaching from Coach Garcia and the lessons learned throughout the years of competing. Having a growth mindset along with moving from being a hard working coachable athlete to one that competed against himself to be better allowed me to achieve my "*Jump and Shout*" moment of being a state champion.

Sign that was posted on the highway as vehicles entered Springfield, IL. Now hangs at Lanphier H.S.'s Memorial Stadium.

When I reflect on all the lessons learned, they all fall into one of four categories or what I call the four Musts: physical, technical, tactical and mental/emotional/social.

The <u>physical</u> refers to anything dealing with an athlete's body. The most obvious is the training one does during and outside of practice to prepare for competition. This refers to conditioning, fitness, weight training, speed agility, or anything else to improve athletic performance. The physical portion of training is usually the one area that coaches prepare for the athlete. What many miss in this category is the importance of nutrition and recovery. Both can prime the body for the athlete to be physically at his/her best and minimize injuries. Recovery in this case does not refer to recovery from an injury, but does refer to recovery after intense exercise. The amount of sleep and proper nutrition can enhance an athlete's physical recovery from a workout while also helping prevent injury. During my competitive years my parents helped with nutrition, but it was on me to get enough sleep. It is tough for student-athletes when balancing school work and, for some, a work schedule. It takes a lot of planning and responsibility to ensure that you are at your best. During my senior year I included icing after competitions or really hard workouts as a prevention and to help with recovery.

The technical category is the skill portion of your practice (team or individual). This is where the "why" of what and how you are doing in practice is answered. It is essential to become an expert at the skill that is needed for your sport. The more you learn from experts the better and more efficient in movements/positions you will become. In order to become a technical expert in your sport, have someone take a video of you and analyze it based on the information you are learning. This allows for more in-depth conversations with your coach and for purposeful training. Purposeful training also leads to improved confidence because you know you are getting better at overcoming your weaknesses.

Having a great understanding of the tactical side of your game or event will make you a great competitor. The understanding of the tactical side refers to the rules of the game/event and the different philosophies tied to it. This places you, as an athlete, in the best situation to be successful because you know how to be proactive in a competition, and how to respond to the competition's actions. The more you know the history of the sport and become an expert at the tactical side of the competition the more you understand the "why" of what you are doing. This will again build confidence.

Many times the coach is the expert and assists in this area. But, in the heat of competition the coach may not have time to respond to those tactics. An athlete must often respond in the right way to put themselves in the best situation to succeed. The more you know about your sport as an athlete the better in game response you will have. A great example of this is when and why I would pass a height or not during a high jump competition. Passing a height may give me an advantage at certain points in the competition where other times it would not. The more I know about high jump and the rules the better decision I can make. Here is another example I collect a rebound in a basketball game and the ball is in my hands. Should I push the ball up the court fast or should I walk the ball up and play more of a half-court game. Again, when there is a good understanding of the game of basketball, the best decision can be made in that moment.

The <u>mental/emotional/social</u> is the most complex of the "Musts" and is many times not focused on. The mental side is where an athlete must be "in the moment" for practice and competitions. It is very easy to get distracted by other things going on in school, family dynamics, social life, or even the attention that comes along with success. Mentally and emotionally, it is very important to be driven, committed, determined, and focused in on the process. The largest challenge is trying to balance the social part of your life with trying to achieve your "*Jump and Shout*" moment. Finding time to be with friends is important to your happiness and relaxation, but there will be times when a decision to rest, work out, or focus on your goals will have to come before or instead of social time. The decision to be disciplined or to relax will be a hard decision to make.

It is very complex to have all four "Must" areas balanced at a very high level, but it is doable with the characteristics of drive, commitment, determination, and both the growth and champion mindsets (mindset X2). If one or more of the "musts" are out of balance, it will be hard to achieve your "*Jump and Shout*" moment. It is easier to let one area slide and be just good enough, but to be a champion you have to be committed to make decisions and actions to ensure each "Must" is at the highest level. Very few people achieve their "*Jump & Shout*" moment, because they are not willing to put in the effort, or do not follow through with the discipline to do so.

Working hard is not the same as working for your "*Jump and Shout*" moment(s). Most people work hard, but to achieve your "*Jump and Shout*" moment you must be prepared to not just work hard but to have the mindset of competing everyday against yourself in order to be better prepared for your moment. It is not easy to maintain the four "Musts" consistently. It is important to understand that some tough or bad days will occur. How you deal with those days will be important. You will want to have more consistent days balancing the four "Musts." Some find it tough to just have them balanced throughout a whole season. It is not easy but working to balance the "Musts" even on your tough days will make you more successful in the long run. This can be achieved by having what I term the four characteristics that are needed to achieve a high level of success. The four characteristics are: drive, commitment, determination, and mindset X2. The final chapters will focus on these characteristics.

Reader self-reflection:

1. What are your strength's and weaknesses according to the physical "Must?"
2. What are your strength's and weaknesses according to the technical "Must?"
3. What are your strength's and weaknesses according to the tactical "Must?"
4. What are your strength's and weaknesses according to the social/emotional "Must?"
5. How will you go about improving the areas that are weaknesses and maintaining the areas that are strengths?
6. How balanced are your "Musts?"
7. If they are unbalanced even just a little, how might you go about balancing them better?

Chapter 9

Characteristic One: Drive

Over the years, my dad and I have been asked multiple times what it takes to be highly successful or elite in sports. I recently heard the parents of two highly recruited athletes being asked the same thing. The answer to the question is simple, but the work is not! Very few are actually willing to put in the work to be highly successful. Some would say that there is not a silver bullet to being highly successful in sports. I would agree that there is not one program or coaching philosophy that will automatically lead someone to be highly successful in athletics. I would also say that what works for one athlete may not work for another athlete. What I have found through my own experiences as an athlete, coach, son of a coach, and parent is that there are four characteristics that a person must develop or possess to be successful in sports and in life.

The four characteristics to achieve high success as an individual are: Drive, Commitment, Determination, and Mindset X2. Everything else will fill in the gaps or add to these four. There are other things that are important like discipline, skill/technical work, process over outcome, coachability, confidence, and competing at the highest level possible, but these all crumble or are not fully utilized if these four characteristics are not in place. If the four characteristics are not in place, an athlete's potential cannot reached and success is ultimately not met. Each individual has his or her physical athletic ability based on their DNA and physical makeup. Each individual is different. But what cannot change is possessing/developing these four characteristics and the skills of the sport you participate in.

The characteristics of drive are defined for this purpose as to how bad one wants something, how motivated one is, and how passionate one is. Drive is the "why" behind your choices of what you choose to do or not do. Without a great amount of drive, high level achievement and high success are not reached. Without drive, potential is not fulfilled. Think about how many times you have seen gifted athletes physically not be highly successful or win the big game. The reason is because they did not have the drive to put in the amount of work needed and did not prepare the best they could. A very small percentage of athletes have the amount of drive to put in the work to be highly successful.

Drive can be developed. The drive to be highly successful comes from loving what you do, having passion for the sport, and wanting to be the best. High success will follow. Athletes participate in sports for a variety of reasons: because it is fun, their friends do it, they want something to do, they like the coach, or their parents want them to do it. If one of these reasons is why the athlete chooses to play in the sport, then they will not have the drive to be highly successful. This does not mean they would not be successful or happy. They still could be those things, but the likelihood that they would be highly successful or reach an elite is minimal until the drive to be the best at the sport is developed or realized. In order to have this level of drive an athlete must have a passion and a love for his or her sport. That level of passion along with a high level of drive may be uncovered or developed at different rates. It is on each individual athlete's time frame. Many athletes will never have the passion or the level of drive that is necessary to be highly successful at his or her sport.

Recently, I read a story about a high school senior who was having an amazing fall season and starting to get recruited because of his fall performance. The coach said that he was like a different kid who showed up in June at summer work outs. All of a sudden the kid was more motivated, putting in extra work, and playing harder. The kid said the difference was because he was driven to leave a lasting legacy and wanted to play in college. He took ownership. The drive must come from the athlete. No one can give it to them or force it upon the them.

Parents cannot want it more than the athlete. I struggled with this for many years. I wanted my kids to want it like I did, but what I found is that the kids will only progress so much without an innate drive. To be highly successful, it had to be something that they wanted. If kids are practicing, working out, or playing because their parent wants them too, they will not have the drive to take their work to the level that is needed to be highly successful. The athlete will just do enough so he or she is not in trouble or letting someone down. Plus, the feeling of never being good enough will be felt. Parents, if your kids don't have the drive to be highly successful but they are just happy participating in sports then let them be happy and enjoy watching your kids be happy.

It is easy to spot a kid with a level of drive versus a kid who does not. A kid with a high level of drive not only does extra work but also does the work without being told or asked.

T.J. being recognized at a basketball for winning a state championship with his parents in order of left to right (Jim, T.J., Coach Garcia, Marilyn)

Many times, a highly driven kid must be told to stop, take a break, or it is time to go home and be done for the day. A highly driven kid is one who plays harder in practice and games than other kids. A highly driven kid is one that does not short work outs and does not stop when enough is done. The highly driven kid makes sport and practice almost a way of life and refuses to be average.

I have witnessed kids with a high level of drive when they were younger and then lose it by the time they were older. I also have witnessed kids who were not driven at all when they were younger, and all of a sudden, they become highly driven late in their high school career. Each kid is different, and if allowed and supported, they will find what they are highly passionate about in time. As an eighth grader, I was very driven to be a college basketball player. However, as a junior in high school, that drive shifted to becoming a state champion in the high jump and earning a college scholarship in track and field. The sad truth is that kids can quickly lose their passion and drive based on poor experiences or being excessively pushed by a parent and/or coach. Athletes can also lose their passion if the competitive challenge is far too easy or far too hard. It is fine to change sports and/or passions if the athlete is having more fun with another sport or activity. This results in the athlete being more driven, more successful, and happier.

There is a fine line for a parent and a coach in pushing and being excessive. If an athlete is allowed to find a better playing opportunity every time they are pushed or challenged, they will miss out on life skills such as working through adversity. Sports can teach us multiple life skills that can be used later in life. If your child does not have the high level of drive, let him or her enjoy playing the sport and learn hard work. If your child has developed a high level of drive, then find the right challenge for continued improvement.

Elite athletes that are highly successful are also those who have an elite level of drive to be the best. An athlete must take ownership of his or her drive. If forced upon them or if they are doing something because they are scared, the drive necessary to be elite will not be reached. Drive is what separates the average from good and the good from great.

High success to me is when someone achieves his or her dreams and goals. When it comes to sports, some may say high success is winning or placing in state or competing in college.

Some also would include being named all-state and/or all-conference in high school or even the step further of competing in college. All of those are great and can be used to measure success. For me, high success is being consistently excellent at whatever you choose to do. A student-athlete must define what high success means to him or her. For drive to be focused, purposeful, and have the greatest impact, high success and/or excellence must be defined and described.

Reader self-reflection:

1. How often do you go and work on your sport by yourself?
2. How often do you enjoy your practices/games?
3. Do you have to be asked to do more?
4. How would you define success? What does it look like? What does it feel like? What does it sound like?
5. How do you know if you reached success?
6. How will you maintain success?

Chapter 10

Characteristic Two: Commitment

Once a student-athlete has the drive or the motivation to achieve high success or excellence, the characteristic of commitment helps put the drive into action. This is where the rubber meets the road; this is the work. Commitment is how often one is willing to work to achieve his or her goal. It is easy to have the drive or the want, but it is really hard to actually do the work.

According to schlolarshipstats.com, 7.6 percent of high school varsity athletes will play their sport at some level of college with only 1.8 percent of high school seniors playing at the NCAA Division 1 level[1]. Therefore, most athletes (92.4 percent) will not play in college and this will include many who stated they wanted to. It is just as difficult to win a state title. The purpose of sharing this information is not to discourage anyone; it is just to share the reality and the difficulty of playing sports in college or even winning a state title. As an athlete and a coach I have heard many kids say they want to win a state title or go compete athletically in college. These athletes had the drive and many worked hard, but were not committed to the level that was needed.

T.J. Jumper at the Big Ten Conference Meet. left to right (Meet official Connie Johnson, T.J. Jumper, T.J.'s wife Laura Jumper)

There are different levels of commitment that an athlete can possess. Since there is a very low percentage of those actually making it to college, it is highly important to not only have the drive, but to have the highest level of commitment as well. Working hard in organized practice is great, but if someone wants to win a state title or play in college being committed to working individually on his or her game outside of practice on a weekly basis is needed. Usually these individuals are also committed to what some have called a "championship mindset" in everything in their life. They are committed to getting good grades, being a good person, eating right, getting a good night's sleep, becoming an expert in their sport, and even working out extra. These are also athletes who need to be reminded that they need to take a break to mentally and physically recover. These are the ones with an elite level of drive and commitment, the ones who will have a better shot competing in college athletics.

Athletes with this drive and commitment are also the individuals who are the most successful. They have ownership and are not required to work out by others, including parents and coaches, because they do it on their own accord. These athletes are given choices and guidance but are the ones that take the action. When athletes are directly told they need to do extra workouts their purpose and the focus of the athlete is limited resulting in limited levels of success.

Reader self-reflection:

1. What do you want to do after high school? What are your goals?
2. What do you think commitment looks like on a daily basis? What does commitment look like on a weekly basis?
3. What is your plan to achieve your goals?
4. What are you committed to do to meet your goals? Short-term and long-term?
5. What changes do you need to make to meet those goals?

Chapter 11

Characteristic Three: Determination

The third characteristic to achieve high success is determination. Determination is how bad do you want it and what will you do to get it. Determination is an important characteristic to possess for high success because everyone goes through challenges and setbacks. How you bounce back from the challenges and setbacks will have a huge impact on the level of success that is achieved. Therefore, determination is the power to overcome, exhibit grit, and persevere. Angela Duckworth who wrote *Grit: The Power of Passion and Perseverance,* mentioned that grit is displayed when you struggle or your progress is slowed, and you work to overcome what is occurring to continue to work towards your goal[2].

High success is being consistently excellent. Every athlete deals with setbacks and distractions that may take away from the ability to reach excellence or maintain consistency at a high level. These range from injuries, being sick, personal and family situations, social events, relationships with teammates/coaches, and coaching decisions, to just name a few. The difference between being good, successful, and highly successful is how an athlete responds to these setbacks.

T.J. after not jumping well in a college track meet.

The easy path is to let it negatively impact you by allowing it to bring down your confidence, have a negative mindset, or even impact your commitment to be better. The best thing an athlete can do in setback situations is to increase drive and commitment. This type of mindset and work ethic reflects someone who has a high degree of determination and would not be held back from reaching their dreams and goals.

Two quotes that resonate with the characteristic of determination are:

1. An American essayist, lecturer, philosopher, abolitionist, and poet Ralph Waldo Emmerson said, "For the resolute and determined there is time and opportunity."

2. A quote from American poet Adrienne Rich, "Courage is not defined by those who fought and did not fall, but by those who fought, fell and rose again."

To me, resolute means that when an athlete faces setbacks and distractions, one needs to have courageous and unwavering determination to continue towards consistent excellence. As an athlete, you must have courageous determination when you face setbacks and distractions. The greatest thing about overcoming a setback is that you realize how tough you really are, and the experience can build your confidence.

Reader self-reflections:

1. What are some setbacks and distractions that may occur in your life?
2. How will you respond to those setbacks and distractions?
3. How will you respond to setbacks and distractions that you have not planned for?
4. Who can be a person that could support and encourage you in overcoming those setbacks and distractions? Refer back to chapters 2 and 3.

Chapter 12

Characteristic Four: Mindset X2

The first three characteristics were drive, commitment, and determination. The fourth characteristic is mindset X2. Mindset X2 refers to growth mindset and champion mindset. Growth mindset is how you view life. Champion mindset is how you act and carry yourself. The reason this fourth characteristic is termed Mindset X2 is because you cannot fully have one mindset without the other to be highly successful and reach your goals.

Growth mindset was coined and made widely known by Dr. Carol Dweck in her 2007 book *Mindset: The New Psychology of Success.* According to Dr. Dweck, there are two types of mindsets: fixed and growth. A fixed mindset is the perspective that things are unchangeable. An example would be that you were born this way. A growth mindset is having the perspective that things can be improved and learned [3]. Way too often, athletes, parents, the media, and coaches focus entirely on wins and losses, and awards. When winning is the main and only focus there will be extreme ups and downs emotionally with very limited improvement. The reason for the limited improvement is because the focus is on the end result and also on the completion. This is the fixed mindset.

According to Dr. Jim Afremow's 2013 book, *The Champion's Mind,* a fixed mindset makes it hard to have courageous determination to overcome setbacks and distractions. It also negatively impacts an athlete's drive and confidence because of the focus on outcomes and extrinsic factors. Many times the end result, even if the game is won or a goal achieved, will result in the feeling of emptiness because the athlete will not know where to go next according to Afremow [4].

Whereas an athlete who focuses on continual improvement will have a greater sense of achievement, confidence, and be more likely to have courageous determination. Dr. Dweck [5] calls this growth mindset whereas Dr. Afremow [6] refers to this as the mastery approach. When the emphasis is placed on the process of getting better and continual learning there will be a great deal of improvement over time and the winning will take care of itself. The focus is on oneself and what you as the athlete can control. This will create a balance emotionally because there will be a purpose to everything. It will also create a purposeful drive and commitment. This is the difference from winning some of the time to becoming consistently excellent.

The champion mindset is the second part of mindset X2. It is carrying yourself with confidence and putting into action drive, commitment, determination, and the growth mindset in all areas of life. Therefore, without the growth mindset an athlete cannot have a champion mindset. The champion mindset is working to become the "best" you. It is working to reach your potential in everything you do which is not possible without a growth mindset and a desire to get better. Far too often, an athlete will only have the champion mindset for his or her sport but does not have it in everyday life. They will shortchange, cut corners, or do what is easiest instead of having the four characteristics.

T.J. Jumper being inducted into the Springfield Sports Hall of Fame. Pictured with his wife and daughters

Instead, the athlete will turn it on and off, which is the opposite of the champion mindset. An athlete's mind, emotions, and body don't work well when you try to turn it on and off. It may work sometimes, but eventually it will catch up and the body will not respond in key moments. The body and mind create routines. When the competition is at its greatest and the stress is high, the mind and body are going to go to those routines. If a routine was not created under a champion mindset mistakes will occur and the performance will result in an athlete losing the big competition and, most of all, not reaching their potential as an athlete or a person. When watching individual and teams compete it is easy to see who may have cut a corner with one or more of the four "Musts", or who is not implementing the characteristics of high success. In the heat of competition or when the stress is high these are the athletes that falter, don't have the best game, struggle to respond positively, and ultimately lose in the big moment.

The champion mindset is hard work. Few people are willing to put the continual energy and decision-making into living the champion mindset. This is why so few people are consistently excellent. Being continually excellent does not mean you don't make mistakes or don't lose. It also does not mean you are perfect. It means you learn from those situations and improve to be better next time. The growth mindset is implemented. You are driven to be better, you are committed to be better, and you are determined to overcome any challenges to be better each and every day. It is a marathon to get to a level of constant excellent. You must have the mindset X2 in all phases of life. Have it in school, work, relationships, when you interact with others, practice, and in competitions.

CHAPTER 12

Reader self-reflection:

1. What type of mindset, fixed or growth, do you have?
2. If fixed, what needs to change to move to a growth mindset? Beyond a growth mindset, what needs to improve to be even better?
3. How and when do you act with a champion mindset?
4. What areas could you improve on in implementing a champion mindset?

Conclusion

A *"Jump and Shout"* moment is reaching a goal or a dream that you have dedicated yourself to achieving, and when you do so the emotion and the elation overtake you with the feeling of accomplishment. For me, my moment was when I jumped in the air, pumped my fists and yelled. The purpose of this book is to share the lessons I learned and to help others achieve their own *"Jump and Shout"* moment.

Preparing for your *"Jump and Shout"* moment is not a one-time event, but rather a complicated process that will take time. You must first start by identifying your passion and identifying your goal. Then, you must first figure out why your goal is important to you. This is your drive. Then, you must decide how you will reach your goal, i.e. what action steps will you take. Then, you must commit to it. Use your drive and commitment to be so determined that you will overcome any distraction and/or setbacks. After each practice, ask yourself if you have done enough to achieve your *"Jump and Shout"* moment. If your answer is no, then make the changes and keep working. If the answer is yes, you are on the right path. Throughout every day, seek to improve and embody the growth mindset while also carrying yourself with a champion mindset.

The characteristics to achieve high success is about doing

CONCLUSION

them everyday and making them habits. An Australian actor, F.M. Alexander captures this thought with his quote, "People do not decide their futures, they decide their habits and their habits decide their futures." Focus your actions and decisions on implementing the characteristics to achieve high success until they become habits and become ingrained as who you are as a person. Be a person who is driven, committed to doing your best, determined to follow the process to achieve success, and implement mindset X2. Seek to improve with a growth mindset and have a champion's mindset in everything you do. Act and make decisions like a champion would in everything you do.

Once you have the four characteristics of high success consistently in place, then move to balancing the four "Musts": technical, tactical, physical, and social/emotional. The balance of the four "Musts" will increase your confidence and result in consistent excellence as long as you continue to implement the characteristics of high success. Consistent excellence will provide the greatest opportunity for you to achieve your "*Jump and Shout*" moment(s). Now that you have read this book and reflected after each chapter, you should have a pretty good idea of what areas you already do well in and which ones need improvement. Make an action plan using the free worksheet from the Jumper Athletics website, put that plan into action, and go achieve your "*Jump and Shout*" moment.

Notes

CHAPTER 10

1 Patrick O'Rourke. "Scholarship Stats", 2021, https://scholarshipstats.com/.

CHAPTER 11

2 Angela Duckorth, *Grit: The Power of Passion and Perseverance*, London : Ebury Publishing, 2016.

CHAPTER 12

3 Dr. Carol Dweck, *Mindset: The New Psychology of Success*, New York: Penguin Random House LLC, 2007.

4 Dr. Jim Afremow, *The Champion's Mind: How Great Athletes Think, Train, and Thrive*. New York: Rodale Inc., 2013.

5 Dr. Carol Dweck, *Mindset: The New Psychology of Success*, New York: Penguin Random House LLC, 2007.

6 Dr. Jim Afremow, *The Champion's Mind: How Great Athletes Think, Train, and Thrive*. New York: Rodale Inc., 2013.

Also by T.J. Jumper

T.J. Jumper has dedicated his professional career to assisting students to be college and career ready. His ultimate joy is working with kids and helping them achieve success.

Website = http://tjjumper.com/
Twitter = https://twitter.com/TJJumper1
Facebook = https://www.facebook.com/Jumper-Athletics-110783971430309
Instagram = https://www.instagram.com/jumperathletics/

Jumper Athletics

T.J. Jumper founded a company with his wife, Laura, and father, Jim, to assist student-athletes in reaching their dreams and goals. This group of successful former athletes and coaches offer blog posts, camps, clinics, training, consultation, and other services related to assist middle and high school student-athletes. Check out Jumper Athletics at http://tjjumper.com/

www.ingramcontent.com/pod-product-compliance
Lightning Source LLC
Chambersburg PA
CBHW031256290426
44109CB00012B/608